THE 22 UNBREAKABLE LAWS OF SELLING

/// JON E. HORTON \\\

Copyright © 2013 Jon E. Horton
All rights reserved.

ISBN: 1480133825
ISBN-13: 9781480133822

Library of Congress Control Number: 2012919834
CreateSpace, Independent Publishing Platform
North Charleston, South Carolina

ABOUT THE AUTHOR

JON E. HORTON HAS WORKED IN SALES, MARKETING AND CONSULTING FOR MORE THAN FOUR DECADES. Through his extensive experience in the field of telecommunications, he has been able to apply his sales expertise to form strong partnerships with executives from a wide variety of industries. He has distilled his years of work into the rules and vignettes found in *The 22 Unbreakable Laws of Selling*.

Jon is a Lexington, Kentucky native. He attended Indiana University where he earned both undergraduate (B.A.) and law (J.D.) degrees. He currently lives with his wife (Rebecca) and two cats (Coco and Owen) in the Phoenix metropolitan area. Jon also has a son (Jon) and two grandchildren (Cade and Chloe).

TABLE OF CONTENTS

Introduction I
1. The Law of Self 1
2. The Law of Organization 7
3. The Law of Knowledge 15
4. The Law of Numbers 21
5. The Law of Qualification 27
6. The Law of Attrition. 33
7. The Law of Decision Makers 39
8. The Law of Gatekeepers 45
9. The Law of Needs 51
10. The Law of Presentations 57
11. The Law of Practice 65
12. The Law of Ears. 71
13. The Law of Attention 77
14. The Law of Persistence 83
15. The Law of 80-20 87
16. The Law of Flexibility 93
17. The Law of Negotiation 99
18. The Law of Closing. 105
19. The Law of Expectations 111
20. The Law of Reliability 115
21. The Law of Gifts. 121
22. The Law of Managers. 127

INTRODUCTION

I'm certain you have heard, probably many times, someone described as "a natural born salesman." You likely nod in agreement and marvel at the skill set possessed by the person under discussion, never pausing to consider the implications of accepting the comment as being accurate.

But this assertion, if true, has potentially crushing consequences for anyone aspiring to a career in sales. Because if, indeed, good sales people are "naturally born", then successful sellers result from genetic accidents and applicants for this vocation need to first check their personal genome maps. At best, those blessed with good selling genes are significantly more likely to succeed – at worst, those without the correct genetic markers are doomed to fail.

It is beyond the scope of this book (and way above my pay grade) to analyze the volumes of research conducted in support of either nature or nurture. But you may safely assume that I would not bother promulgating *The 22 Unbreakable Laws of Selling* if I didn't believe that virtually anyone can excel in the sales arena. During my tours of duty as a Sales Manager, I witnessed many rookies who were at first brutally bad sellers blossom into so-called "killers." How? They learned their craft!

To be sure, some people appear to master the laws of selling more quickly than others. But I contend this process has nothing to do with nature. Rather, the acquisition of good sales habits simply requires approaching the subject matter with the right mind set. Would be sellers must have a willingness to study and practice, to learn from mistakes and accept criticism, to dismiss ego and pride and to work hard. The fact that you have purchased this book suggests that your head is in a good place.

There are fundamental sales practices – rules, if you will – presented here as laws that, if strictly followed, will produce excellent sales results. In many cases, these laws are neither natural nor intuitive. For instance, that "natural born salesman" is often characterized as "having the gift of gab." In truth, the best salespeople are those who are good listeners rather than good talkers.

So, take heart fledgling sellers. Learn your lessons (laws) well and you will enjoy a long and prosperous career in sales.

In closing, I'll take a shot at answering those of you wondering why I settled on precisely 22 Unbreakable Laws. My response must include nods to Reis and Trout who greatly enhanced my career with their 22 Immutable Laws of Marketing and to a dear friend of mine who has maintained for decades that 22 is the luckiest number in the world. But the fact is that, as I distilled years of experience to generate these laws, it became apparent that fifteen was not enough and thirty was too many. Please read my book and see if you don't agree that 22 is a very good number.

Your comments are more than welcome. Please send them to **Jon@JonEHorton.com**.

Jon E. Horton
2012
Peoria, Arizona

ONE

THE LAW OF SELF

You can't make this stuff up!

As a brand new salesman, still very much wet behind the ears, I was handed a box of business cards and no active clients. None. Zero. Zilch. Nada.

"The world is your oyster," my manager told me. "There are hundreds of potential customers out there – your job is to find them and sell them."

So, for me, prospecting and cold calling were synonyms. I was both naïve enough to believe I could be successful (I was correct) and aggressive enough to go after it with a vengeance, determined to leave no stone unturned in my quest to build a giant account list.

One of my first bright ideas was to get involved with the local Chamber of Commerce – an organization certain to be teeming with wealthy prospects, all anxious to do business with me. Armed with membership under my employer's umbrella, I added that group's next mixer to my calendar.

Upon arrival, I made straight for the bar, thinking this would be a good place to meet people (while building my social courage). The middle-aged man behind me in line was, candidly, pot-bellied and wore wrinkled khaki pants, an equally wrinkled navy jacket and a pair of what most closely resembled bowling shoes.

Undaunted, I boldly introduced myself and, upon learning that his name was Larry, I asked, "What line of work are you in?"

"I'm a car salesman," Larry replied in a monotone voice. "I sell Buicks and Chevrolets."

"Oh," I said, bravely disguising my unhappy realization that he was not a good prospect for me. "And, how is business these days?"

"Up and down," he muttered. "It just depends on whether I get lucky with who I catch out on the car lot."

Anxious to terminate this conversation but determined to do so with grace, I said, "Well, let me have one of your business cards in case I'm looking for a new car."

He fumbled through keys and change in his pocket and finally produced a creased card that only displayed the name of the dealership. "You can write my name on the back. It's Larry," he said and, thankfully, walked away.

Beginning to sense that this prospecting thing was more challenging than I had anticipated, I sipped on my drink and silently let several people come and go from the bar. I was shaken out of my reverie by a gentleman who was introducing himself to me. I say "gentleman" because he was nicely groomed, wore an expensive looking but conservatively grey suit and smiled warmly while looking me in the eye during his greeting.

"My name is William," he said comfortably, "But my friends call me Bill."

"Hi Bill," I responded, not realizing I had already elected to be counted as one of his friends. "I'm Jon. What do you do for a living?"

"I work in transportation solutions," he said.

"I see." I was impressed although I wasn't sure why. "Is that a government position?"

"No," he explained. "I actually work one-on-one with individuals. Here's my card."

I immediately noticed the embossed Mercedes-Benz logo and blurted, "Oh, you sell cars!"

"Well," he smiled patiently, "My clients may ultimately acquire a vehicle through me. But, that will only happen after we have thoroughly assessed their needs as well as their resources and made an informed decision to go forward."

Bill, of course, was not a good prospect for me. Nevertheless, I'm proud to say that he did become a good friend.

I didn't, in fact, meet any good prospects that day. I did, however, learn two valuable lessons. First, Chamber of Commerce mixers are good places to meet other sellers. Second, I no longer wanted anyone to think of me as only a salesperson. Thanks to Bill, I wanted to be more.

So, what do you want to be when you grow up?

During one of the most painful job interviews I have ever endured – I was the one being interviewed – my potential employer asked me, "What do you want to have written on your epitaph?" I thought the question was far too esoteric, particularly since I didn't know then (and still do not) which answer would be right and which would be wrong. In the scheme of life, being remembered as a wonderful child or parent probably takes precedence over a job. But, in the context of selling, the question helps make my point.

Since you are reading my book, it appears you have decided on a career in sales. But, if the legend on your tombstone read, "A Great Salesperson," would you be satisfied? Even if true, would those words adequately summarize what you did with your work life? Is that how you would describe yourself? More importantly, is that how your clients would characterize your relationships with them?

This **isn't** about semantics in the sense that these are not trick questions and they require only straightforward responses. Simple as they may be, however, your answers will illuminate the path of your career in sales.

This **is** about semantics in the sense that the key to this entire exercise is the definition of "salesperson" – not just any definition but your definition. Depending on perspective, the term could be a pejorative description ("a peddler") or high praise ("a partner") and the next few pages are about choosing the latter.

I don't mean to suggest that describing yourself as a "salesperson" is a bad thing. It is my intention, however, to insist that you carefully consider what the word means to you and the corresponding implications for your approach to your chosen profession.

Abiding by The Law of Self requires all would be sellers to complete a three step process. They must first define, with specificity, what being a salesperson means to them. The next step is to identify, again in detail, the work activities required to attain the status they have described. Finally, they have to internalize the commitment that will turn that level of performance into habit.

The most challenging step is the first one. When asked to describe the kind of salesperson they want to be, typical seller responses would include "a good one" or "a successful one" or "a respected one" to which I would respond "sure" or "yes" or "absolutely". Each of these is a seller attribute to which, undoubtedly, we all aspire.

The problem with these answers is that they provide virtually no guidance for achieving step two. The desire to be a "successful" salesperson is closer to being a wish than a call to action. Rather than let you continue to scratch your head in search of better responses, allow me to shift your focus.

Somewhat ironically, the most positive and useful definitions of a "salesperson" come not from the minds of sellers but rather from the perspectives of customers! Think about it. It is, after all, clients who possess the power to determine whether a seller is "good" or "successful" or "respected". It only makes sense, then, to listen closely to what customers have to say and use their words in the "self" portrait that is the subject of this chapter.

Clients may use many words to describe the attributes they value from a salesperson but my earlier use of "partner" is certainly a prime example. This concept suggests that the customer views the seller as a peer, a co-worker making an important contribution to the success of the client's business. This salesperson contributes industry perspective and ideas while delivering affordable solutions to performance challenges and goals.

Armed with this or a similarly customer-centric idea of what it means to be a salesperson, step two becomes relatively straightforward. In fact, perceptive readers have recognized that the job of identifying required work activities is already complete! Hello!? The book you are currently reading – *The 22 Unbreakable Laws of Selling* – delineates precisely the action steps necessary for sellers to develop "partner" relationships with their customers. Just follow me to the promised land!

The final leg in The Law of Self process requires that salespeople make a commitment to adjust their performance based on what they have learned. Readers will find this admonition to be a recurring theme throughout this book. I believe this repetition is necessary – not because I think you are stubborn or stupid – but because I'm certain you are human and, absent relentless vigilance, natural tendencies will replace learned behavior.

I regret that I don't know the original source of this quote but someone who should be famous once said, "If it were easy, everybody would do it!" Being a superior salesperson is hard work and requires a very special commitment.

So, with The Law of Self behind you, your career in sales is ready to take flight. You have a clear picture of the salesperson you want to be, you hold in your hand the 22 keys to success and you are committed to making it happen. Whether you have been employed as a seller for a day or a decade, today really is the first day of your new sales life!

TWO

THE LAW OF ORGANIZATION

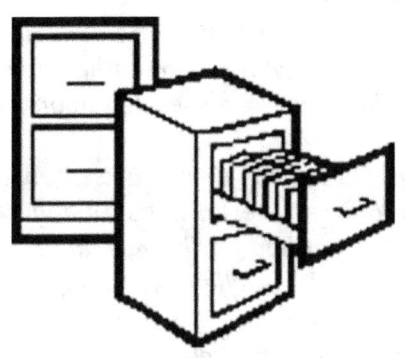

My sales cubicle was directly across from that of a new hire so I had a bird's eye view of his activity from day one. I liked him immediately. It was hard not to given his relentless, infectious smile and boundless energy. He suffered through completing required new employee paperwork and some rudimentary orientation, chomping at the bit to get out of the office and start calling on potential clients. In a matter of days, armed with a stack of sales brochures and freshly minted business cards, he set off to conquer the world.

I saw very little of him after that but I knew he was enjoying early success. He would stop by the office late each afternoon, just long enough to write up the business he had closed that day and the pile of orders he submitted was truly impressive.

Although the new seller was rarely in evidence, within a couple of weeks his desk had become a beehive of activity. Between our Business Manager, Production Director and Sales Assistant, someone was almost always hovering near his cubicle, sometimes leaving handwritten notes and other times just checking to see if he was in, clearly exasperated upon learning that he was not there.

The reasons behind all these visits soon became known throughout our offices. The Business Manager was following up on sales orders that had not been counter-signed by clients or looking for required new client credit applications that were never submitted. The Production Director needed the details necessary to comply with the sellers hastily written orders and the Sales Assistant was trying to pass along multiple messages from angry clients who were never contacted again after tentatively placing an order.

Sadly, our new seller just couldn't keep track of the follow-up details associated with new contracts and new clients. It's almost anti-climactic to report that he was terminated in less than 60 days and this story would almost be funny if the result weren't so tragic.....tragic and unnecessary. A seller of only ordinary intelligence should realize that every business has detailed protocols which must be followed and, with that recognition, should understand that the requisite organizational habits can be mastered by anyone with the appropriate commitment.

I have tried to order the chapters of this book in a way that makes sense with related topics positioned next to each other. Nevertheless, in spite of my efforts, many of the chapters could be juxtaposed without sacrificing significant comprehension for the reader.

Such is not the case for The Law of Organization which, in any configuration, must be a priority. Organization is critical because, quite simply, the other laws cannot be followed consistently if a seller is not meticulously organized. Good organizational skills are the cornerstone of good selling practices.

Being organized eliminates the need for sellers to remember the next step and insures that all elements of the selling process will be executed in a timely fashion. To be sure, having a good memory is a useful attribute for a seller to have. But memory alone is insufficient for the many tasks associated with being a successful salesperson. If it had been my intention for readers to memorize the contents of this book, I would have authored The 3 Unbreakable Laws of Selling. Unfortunately, good selling practices cannot be summarized in such a conveniently remembered package.

Based on hundreds of interviews I have conducted, sellers almost unanimously cite "better organization" as the personal performance issue they would most like to improve. This comes as no surprise. Even seasoned salespeople are often overwhelmed while trying to juggle a heavy appointment schedule, new business prospecting and existing client follow-up along with new management initiatives.

I am, however, surprised by the difficulty sellers experience when trying to implement the cure for their organizational woes. My readers will likely agree that the "fix" is just too simple to explain an inability or unwillingness to solve the organizational challenge.

My mission to sell you on the simplicity of good organization requires that I first make a rather embarrassing confession. For purposes of writing this book, I have substituted a five syllable, fifty-dollar word – "organization" – for a one syllable, fifty-cent word – "list". (I just wasn't sure I would achieve credibility with a chapter titled, "The Law of List".)

So, there it is. If you want to be organized, make a list. How simple is that?

Well, based on the number of salespeople who fail to master this task, it's apparently not quite that simple. Or, more to the point, it's simple but not easy.

It might be fair to lay blame for this failure at the feet of sellers who stubbornly believe they are capable of substituting their memories for the admittedly mundane but effective method (list) required for good organization. But, to do so would ignore the reality of human nature and the fact that all of us place undue confidence in our ability to remember details.

Consider, for example, the simple concept of making a grocery list. I will wager the price of this book that sometimes you make a list and sometimes you don't. Now, I will bet double or nothing that, on those occasions when you skip the grocery list, you do so because you're certain you can remember everything you need from the store. Finally, I'll parlay my winnings so far into a trifecta, gambling that, without a list, you have gotten home only to realize that you forgot something critical.

If this has ever happened to you – be honest – then your logical response should be to always make a list before going to the grocery. But, I'll bet – please don't let me take any more of your money – that you will grocery shop again without a list. Why? Because it is just that hard to convince yourself that you might forget something so simple.

There is another obstacle to reaching organizational nirvana, one that may be even more daunting than accepting the insufficiency of relying on memory as a substitute for making a list. At least as it relates to sales, the list required for effective organization includes excruciating but exquisite detail.

With apologies for perhaps twisting this metaphor beyond recognition, re-visiting your grocery list may help make my point. For purposes of stocking your refrigerator, simply writing "soft drinks" on your list will suffice. But, an effective seller must break down this straightforward task into its component parts and generate a list that includes carbonated water, caramel color, aspartame, phosphoric acid, natural and artificial flavors, sodium benzoate, caffeine and phenylketonurics. The salesperson's list is a half-page so far with only Diet Dr. Pepper to show for the effort. (God forbid that lasagna is on the menu!)

The ingredients for every step in the selling process are at least this complex – if anything, they are more complicated. Consider, for example, the apparently simple concept of "follow-up after the sale". The most rudimentary elements of acceptable follow-up would certainly include:

- Sending a 'Thank You' note;
- Carefully reviewing the sales order for accuracy;
- Generating a production order;
- Checking on the production schedule (repeatedly);
- Alerting the client to the delivery schedule;
- Confirming client satisfaction;
- Carefully reviewing the invoice for accuracy; and,
- Scheduling the renewal appointment.

These items might suffice for one part of the sales cycle. Then, multiply this list by those required for the other typical elements of the selling process – prospecting, getting an appointment, conducting a client needs analysis, developing a customer-centric plan, generating a written proposal, making the presentation, closing the sale and providing service for existing clients. Finally, bear in mind that all of these lists are required for every single account managed by a seller which, depending on the industry, could add a factor ranging from ten to one-hundred.

The bottom line is that a good salesperson's list will include hundreds of tasks and the prospect of collating all these items must be somewhat intimidating to a new seller. You may, in fact, be asking yourself, "Is all this detail really necessary?"

Simply stated, the answer is a resounding, "Yes!" It is impossible to prioritize the myriad facets of superior selling because they are all integral parts that combine seamlessly to produce the sales mosaic. Like a jigsaw puzzle with a missing piece, the seller who skips a single step in the sales process will have that oversight embarrassingly exposed.

Attention to detail, however tedious, is required for success in sales and mastering The Law of Organization demands a commitment of the highest order. A superior seller will trust nothing (sales activities) to memory and will, instead, rely entirely on a meticulously crafted list.

For those willing and able to make this commitment, there is a rewarding silver lining. Virtually every nuance of the remaining 20 Unbreakable Laws of Selling can be – no, will be – mastered by simply integrating the tenets into a seller's organizational list.

Finally, armed with a commitment to organization, every salesperson must adopt a system that facilitates execution of all activities on their list. Since each step in the sales process (with a distinct process for each individual client) has a different due date, it only makes sense to use a calendar-based system and there are many from which to choose.

I actually considered devoting several paragraphs to describing and extolling the virtues of technologically efficient alternatives like Outlook or my personal favorite, a Cloud-based system that distributes a calendar schedule across multiple smart devices. But, in truth, there is no inherent reason that a committed (if digitally challenged) seller cannot perform equally as well with a good pen and a bound paper Daytimer. So, I'll leave the choice of medium up to you. There are, however, some organization (list) practices which should be followed under any circumstances.

> 1. New sales activities should be plotted on the calendar at the absolute earliest practicable time, even if the task isn't scheduled for completion for months. For example, making the call for a renewal appointment should be added to the calendar the day the initial sale is made, thereby insuring that this follow-up item will be done in a timely fashion;
> 2. The calendar should be reviewed daily at close of business. Completed items should be checked off and consideration given as to whether finishing one task gives rise to a new activity which needs to be scheduled;
> 3. List items not completed on the day scheduled MUST be re-scheduled immediately although it's acceptable to move them forward by days or even weeks. The critical mantra is this – if an activity was important enough to get on the list, the task must stay on the list until completed; and,
> 4. Spend a little time making sure your organization is organized. In the interest of efficiency, try and group similar tasks together each day. Also, follow that old adage that directs you to do first those things that you want to do least.

Because you purchased this book, it's fair to assume that you aspire to become a successful seller. Perhaps you were attracted to this profession in the belief that you have the right personality for sales or because your good work can produce a handsome income or you're convinced that selling will be fun. Whatever your motivation, I applaud your decision because I believe the sales profession is a high calling. However.....

If The Law of Organization has in any way dampened your enthusiasm, you might want to give this book to a friend and consider a different line of work. Selling should be both fun and financially rewarding but it is not easy. And, if you are unwilling or unable to master organizational skills, your sales career is doomed to failure. Think about it.

I hope you're still with me and, if you are, let's turn the page.

THREE

THE LAW OF KNOWLEDGE

For a birthday or some other date of note, my sister-in-law gave us one of those digital picture frames. After getting it loaded with every available picture from both of our computers, we quickly became addicted to the slideshow, often stopping midstep to watch the transitions for two or three minutes.

At some point, it dawned on me that this experience would be improved if we could view the same images on our big-screen television. Our 60-inch plasma, however, was several years old (pre-Internet connection) and I wasn't sure it was possible to marry digital pictures with the TV. To my delight, I discovered the "display photos" section in the television manual and, with the aid of a flashlight, I found the appropriate memory card slot on the TV.

The next day, I dropped off my cat for his annual "free" gum examination and teeth cleaning. (The salesperson who conned me into signing this pet insurance policy could have written this book – but that's another story.) With time to kill, I decided to run in to the major office supply retail store next door and pick up a memory stick to use with my television.

I found the section where the digital devices were displayed but was immediately stumped by the variety of sizes (memory), shapes and descriptions available. Clearly needing help, I finally flagged down a clerk and explained my challenge.

"I have a four year-old big screen plasma," I told the salesman, "and I want to get a memory card so I can play a photo slideshow on the TV."

"No-o-o-o problem-o," he chirped, apparently delighted that my perplexed demeanor could be remedied quite easily. "Do you have a lot of pictures?"

Not certain if my collection met that criteria, I decided to be specific. "I currently have about 250 digital pictures and, over the course of time, I will likely double that number."

He instantly grabbed a package from the display wall and cheerily announced, "Super duper! This new 16 gigabyte memory stick will easily hold all your pictures with room to spare and, best of all, it's on sale!"

"That's good," I said, studying his recommendation. "But, this one seems to be bigger than the ones with less memory?"

"Of course," he replied, clearly struggling to be patient with an older, digitally-challenged customer. "Bigger means more memory and – trust me – you'll be glad you have the extra space."

Fresh out of intelligent questions, I did......trust him. After paying the "sale" price, I fairly skipped to my car, nearly forgetting to pick up my cat (who, by the way, did seem to have a brighter smile after his treatment). I couldn't wait to get home and dazzle my wife with my technological victory.

That enthusiasm, unfortunately, was short-lived. It took me less than an hour to rip open the package, copy my pictures from computer to new memory stick, grab a flashlight and determine, with absolute certainty, that the 16 gigabyte toy in my hand would not fit into any of the slots on my television!

My story is nearly over and I assume you'll be pleased to learn that the next hour delivered both a happy ending and an important lesson – for me and you. I immediately returned my purchase to the office supply megastore – the look on my face dissuaded the clerk from charging me a re-stocking fee – and, undaunted by the experience so far, I walked straight to the adjacent electronic superstore to try my luck again.

"I'm trying to find the correct memory stick that will display pictures on my 60-inch plasma," I announced to the salesman who greeted me.

"Okay," he said. "About how many photos are you talking about?"

"Ultimately, I would guess about 500," I replied.

"And," he continued, "How old is your television?"

"I've had it nearly four years," I answered, somewhat surprised by the question. "Why do you ask?"

"Well," he explained, "We have a new 16 gigabyte memory stick that would hold all the pictures you might ever take. However, it will only fit TV models manufactured within the last two years. So, you'll need to get the 8 gigabyte version which *fits your television and will still meet your needs – it will hold approximately 2,000 photos."*

He was right on both counts. I now have a memory stick that works perfectly with my plasma, my wife and I are happy campers and – guess which store will be getting my future business? Product knowledge is a beautiful thing!

Typically, businesses have some sort of structured orientation for new employees although the depth and, therefore, the value of these introductory exercises vary greatly. I have experienced both the highs and lows of this process.

Companies paying only lip service to orientation will greet new hires with a packet of written materials, the highlight of which will be an employee handbook (often out-of-date). There will also be forms (tax withholding, for instance) which the salesperson must immediately complete. The coup de grace will likely be a perfunctory tour of the facilities with unscheduled introductions to company managers who happen to be available.

The more impressive end of the orientation spectrum might feature a PowerPoint presentation designed specifically for new employees with different sections of the slideshow narrated by the appropriate Department Heads. A well-designed program would include detailed descriptions of the correct procedures for all sales tasks including extensive FAQ's. This new hire introduction should conclude with a handout – individual flash drives are the best – that mirrors the entire presentation as well as login instructions for the company's employee web site.

Many, if not most, of my readers have already been hired into sales positions in which case the orientation 'ship' has already sailed. Not to worry – because neither of the introductory exercises described above provides a sufficient information foundation of product knowledge. In truth, superior sellers must design and implement their own orientation programs. The good news is that, regardless of the duration of your current employment, it's never too late to start over.

Charting the activities required to achieve effective product knowledge will be easier if we first identify why and what a good salesperson needs to know. Those answers become fairly straightforward with recognition of one simple premise – the goal of possessing product knowledge is enhancing the ability to service the client.

It is beyond the scope of this book to generate an exhaustive list of every conceivable piece of knowledge a seller should know – The Law of Knowledge simply dictates that top salespeople must be experts in their respective fields. That said, I want to provide enough examples to clearly demonstrate the process.

Service: Which of the products/services you represent will be most useful to your client?

Knowledge: Salespeople must be intimately familiar with every item/option in their product line including how they work, their strengths as well as their limitations. To that end, sellers should schedule adequate time to meet with the person(s) responsible for the design and implementation of the company's products/services. This same practice should be followed for other key departments e.g. accounting and production. (The complete solution to this service challenge also requires knowledge of the client's industry as discussed in the Law of Needs.)

Service: How do your products/services compare to the competition?

Knowledge: Salespeople must know and understand their competition as thoroughly as their own company. The acquisition of this knowledge will require extensive research and should include a review of the competition's marketing and sales materials.

Service: How can your products/services help clients stay ahead of their competition?

Knowledge: Sellers should keep abreast of trends in their own industry but knowledge of new developments doesn't always filter quickly to the sales department. So, salespeople must do their own independent research, most easily achieved by reviewing a variety of trade publications on a weekly basis. You can only share a vision of tomorrow with your client when you know the direction in which your industry is moving. (Again, for the client's perspective, see The Law of Needs.)

Adhering to The Law of Knowledge is hard work, made all the more challenging because the job is never done. There is no static point in time when a seller can say, with a sigh of relief, "Finally, I now have all the knowledge I need!" Rather, maintaining cutting edge knowledge is an ongoing task, one that requires the highest level of commitment.

Throughout these chapters, I present The 22 Unbreakable Laws of Selling as the steps necessary for salespeople to be "effective," "superior" or even "great." Because you invested in this book, I assume you are prepared to make the necessary commitment. So, let's move forward.

FOUR

THE LAW OF NUMBERS

The owner of a small company gave me a six month contract, asking me to do a thorough analysis of his sales operations including my recommendations for changes he should consider. He was concerned about revenues that had either declined or been stagnant, even as his industry was enjoying a strong recovery from the economic meltdown of the late 2000's. To his credit, he entered into our agreement with no sacred cows, giving me total access to the company's business records and instructing all of his employees to make themselves available to meet with me.

The Director of Sales was named Steve and he was the first appointment on my initial visit to corporate headquarters. Experience has taught me that understanding the philosophy and style of management gives good direction to my subsequent investigation of personnel and procedures.

Steve welcomed me with a wide smile that belied his misgivings about my mission. "It's really nice to meet you Jon! I can't wait to learn from your wisdom and insights," he gushed.

He was lying, of course. It was a fib that I expected, one necessitated by the owner's mandate. In reality, he resented my intrusion onto his turf and the very fact of my hiring made him insecure about his job. But, I was prepared for this nervous reception and I knew this wouldn't be the last untruth to pass between him and me.

"It's good to meet you as well, Steve. I've heard great things about the job you are doing," I said glibly. I doubt that he believed me either but, by making nice, we had both announced our intentions to go forward with civility.

We spent several hours together that day and our discussion was, by my design, non-confrontational. I knew Steve would be more likely to be candid with me if he were feeling comfortable, even confident, so I smiled a lot and often nodded agreement with his comments. Besides, my assignment from ownership didn't include challenging his employees face-to-face.

Steve showed me the written promotional sales materials he had created for his staff and he explained the pricing struc-

ture currently in place. He also shared his revenue pacing report which, not surprisingly, was falling well short of budget. At the conclusion of our first meeting, he introduced me to his salespeople with whom I would spend the remainder of the day.

My one-on-one sessions with the individual sellers lasted well into the evening as I peppered each one with the questions I had prepared in advance. While trying to measure their strengths and weaknesses, I was particularly interested to hear Steve's salespeople evaluate their own performances paired with their ideas for improvement.

To a person, all of the sellers were appropriately modest, admitting they could perform better and professing a willingness to take whatever steps would produce improved results. In that context, their suggestions included working "smarter" or "harder" with higher "commitment" and "energy".

The next morning, my final meeting with the Director of Sales held no surprises. I had purposely avoided asking Steve to assess his sellers prior to my own meetings with them, not wanting to let his opinions color my conclusions. When I did finally ask the question, he gave all of his salespeople high marks, expressing confidence that their collective performance was headed in a positive direction.

"Specifically," I asked, "which activities are you tracking? Have you asked your sellers to increase their numbers for prospecting or appointments or presentations or will they be raising prices? What's your plan of attack?"

"No, Jon," he replied in a tone that indicated his profound disappointment with the question. "When you've been doing this as long as I have, you learn that you can't manage people with numbers. My sellers are all unique individuals, I know what makes them tick and I'll use that insight to motivate their performance."

"Wow, that's impressive," I said, smiling to cover my gritted teeth. I shook his hand as I departed and managed to avoid adding, "Good luck with that."

It's usually pretty easy to recognize the takeaway from the vignettes I share to begin each chapter but, with the preceding story, recognizing the moral may be more challenging. Nevertheless, the circumstances and dialogue narrated here are repeated so often, they provide a solid framework for introducing The Law of Numbers.

In the vast majority of my experiences working with sales managers and sales teams, even the smallest hint of reference to numerical calculations elicits a negative response. And, I'm only talking about addition or subtraction – not calculus or trigonometry. Nevertheless, many people in the sales arena are either intimidated by the prospect of working with numbers or offended by the seeming impersonal nature of metrics.

In truth, I believe this avoidance results from a failure to appreciate what a powerful selling tool numbers represent. Just simple arithmetic holds the key that will open the pathway to success, dictating sales activity that is guaranteed – yes, guaranteed – to improve performance. Sellers who understand the direct relationship between straightforward metrics and increased sales will embrace the math and find career security (safety) in numbers.

A basic example – I promised "simple" – should illustrate my point. A review of your calendar for the last few months (see The Law of Organization) will reveal how often making a client presentation results in a sale for you. For the sake of this discussion, let's say you make four sales for every ten presentations you give. (This is called a "closing ratio" but forget the term if it intimidates you.) Armed with these two integers, you now know that making an additional ten presentations will produce four more sales, twenty presentations will give you eight sales and thirty delivers an extra twelve contracts. Guaranteed! How simple is that?!

Perhaps, with this example, you are now ready to have fun with numbers? If that's asking too much, maybe you are at least prepared to consider the possibilities available by extrapolating from the previous exercise? Let's give it a try.

A key component of the closing ratio is the number of client presentations, a metric that is likely dependent upon other activities. A seller's ability to schedule a client presentation, for instance, must often be preceded by a prospect needs analysis meeting which, itself, might require an initial cold call. But, either of these considerations (and many others) lends itself to precisely the same numeric process as the closing ratio I described. How many cold calls are required to produce a needs analysis meeting (an analysis ratio) and how many needs analysis meetings are needed to schedule a client presentation (a presentation ratio)? Well, you get the idea.

The possibilities for manipulating simple numbers to improve selling performance are virtually endless. Salespeople who have pricing flexibility, for example, can easily calculate the change in value of their average contract if they successfully negotiate a higher rate. In fact, none of the myriad numerical considerations available requires more than a high school education. The real challenge is recognizing the value in doing the work.

The superior salesperson will have mastered many topics beyond numbers – there are, after all, twenty-one other chapters in this book. That said, I am very much inclined to agree with the anonymous person who said, "You can't manage it if you can't measure it."

Consider the salespeople I described earlier who hoped to achieve better results by working "harder" or "smarter". How will they know when their mission is complete? Wouldn't they be more likely to enjoy improved performance by simply making more presentations to more prospects?

The logic is inescapable and sellers who refuse to embrace The Law of Numbers will do so to their detriment. They will struggle to find focus for their energies as they strive for platitudes that lack definition.

Conversely, salespeople who collect meaningful numbers, do the simple math processes and allow the results to direct their work activities will enjoy consistent improvement. As a bonus, their performance growth is constantly measured by the same metrics and is clearly apparent to management.

Speaking of management, many of you will find yourselves under the direction of superiors who, like the Director of Sales I encountered, prefer to manage on instinct rather than hard data. Please don't waste your time arguing the point with your boss.

The beauty of The Law of Numbers is that the critical metrics are readily available – no managers required! Sellers can collate the requisite data from their own work files and implement the numbers-directed activity, undetected by management radar. When these surreptitious efforts produce results, smart salespeople will let their superiors take the credit. (See the final chapter in this book – The Law of Managers.)

Some of you will read this chapter and think, "Duh! This math is simple!" Others will continue to resist doing any extra math. To the former I say yes, the math is simple, but the results are more powerful than you can imagine. To the latter I say trust me, making the effort is worth your time and energy. To all my readers I say – DO THE MATH!

There are many skill sets that go into the making of outstanding salespeople but selling is and always will be a numbers game. So, if you're committed to being a winner, get in the game!

FIVE

THE LAW OF QUALIFICATION

Quite a number of years ago, I went online and entered all my telephone numbers on the national (and theoretical) "Do Not Call" list, a process I have repeated several times since. But, as you likely already know, this has turned out to be another well conceived and poorly enforced government program. Telephone solicitors long ago decided it was easier to apologize after the fact than to check the list in advance.

As a result, my phone rings virtually every night, typically in the middle of dinner or a favorite television show, and I am confronted by some functional illiterate trying to sell me something I neither want nor need. Most times I am just plain rude, giving my best effort to make the caller sorry for invading my privacy. But occasionally, my playful (or evil) self takes over and I decide to play along.

I am, after all, in sales and I have something of an obligation to stay abreast of the latest techniques, however predatory they may be. Or, perhaps it's only curiosity that gets the best of me. Either way, I do sometimes allow myself to be a sales guinea pig and such was the case that led to the following dialogue.

"Good evening, sir! Am I speaking with Jon Horton?"

"Yes you are," I replied with a cheerfulness that matched the enthusiasm of the guy calling me.

"Hi Mr. Horton," he enthused. "This is David calling from Sterling Mortgage Savers and the reason for my call is to let you know you have won a free mortgage reduction evaluation from my company!"

"Oh wow," I deadpanned.

"It's true," he continued, happy to assume my response showed genuine interest. "Let me just verify that I have the 'right' Jon Horton. You do own your home there in Arizona, don't you Mr. Horton?"

"I do indeed!" On this particular evening, I could either play along with David or watch an episode of Housewives from Hell with my wife. Given those choices, David had my full attention.

"That's great! Now Mr. Horton.....may I call you Jon?"

"You doesn't has to call me Jon," I quipped, entertaining myself. "But yes, you may call me Jon."

"Thank you. Now Jon, you'll be pleased to know there is absolutely no charge for this evaluation and there's a good chance we're going to save you tens of thousands of dollars! What will you do with all that extra money, Jon?" He paused slightly each time he said my name and I realized he was filling in the blank space on the script from which he was reading.

"Well, I'm sure I could figure out something to do with the money. But honestly, David, I'm not in the market for a mortgage reduction." Although I was enjoying being somewhat mischievous, I wasn't going to lie to the guy.

"Here's the truth...(pause)...Jon," he droned on, ignoring my response and following his prepared monologue. "Sterling Mortgage Savers has been able to put at least an extra $1,000 in the pocket of nearly all our clients!"

"But David," I tried, unsuccessfully, to interrupt.

"You see, mortgage rates have gone way down since the housing bust but the banks have got good people like you locked into paying much higher interest on your loans."

"I know but," I objected, as David continued through his script.

"Their lawyers will try to scare you into making the higher payments. But Sterling Mortgage Savers will show you how to make the lawyers go away!"

"That's nice, David," I fairly shouted, surprised to realize that he had finished his pitch. "But I paid cash for my home so I don't have a mortgage at all."

The silence from his end of the phone was deafening.

"And by the way, David, I got my Law Degree from Indiana University."

The silence was now broken......by a dial tone.

I could as easily have titled this chapter The Law of Prospecting because the process of qualification would certainly fit under the prospecting umbrella. But, although prospecting will be referenced repeatedly in this book – see, for instance, The Law of Attrition in the next chapter – it is mastery of qualification that facilitates multiple aspects of successful selling.

If, for example, sellers have followed the principles from The Law of Organization, I would challenge them to identify the gaps in their schedules which are available to be wasted. The answer, of course, is that those gaps don't exist. If poorly qualified prospects take up space on their calendars, sellers will be, at best, inefficient and, at worst, failures.

The Law of Numbers will be likewise crippled by poor prospect qualification. There are only so many hours in a day, days in a week, weeks in a month, etc. Virtually by definition, a seller's closing ratio will be worse when time is spent trying to sell an unqualified buyer. In truth, every performance metric will suffer.

If I'm doing my job, you're now convinced that qualification is critical and failure to qualify is a bad thing. If that's the case, you'll be relieved to know that effective qualification is really not that difficult. Successful salespeople have simply become adept at asking the right questions. To that end, this chapter's opening vignette is instructive.

David, our hapless telemarketer, actually tried to qualify me when he verified that I was a homeowner (as opposed to merely a tenant). He failed, however, to follow-up with the payoff question – "And Jon, do you have a mortgage on your home?" Duh!

For Sterling Mortgage Savers, not having a mortgage gave me a prospect score of zero and, by not eliciting that information from me, David wasted at least five minutes of his time. Since I'm certain David was being paid on commission, the difference between talking with me for one minute versus five minutes meant less money in his pocket.

So, effectively qualifying prospects is really a fairly straightforward two-step process. First, sellers should carefully define the characteristics that accurately describe a bona fide prospect. Then, they must generate the shortest (efficient) list of questions possible, the answers to which will definitively include or exclude a potential customer.

This is probably the point where you are hoping I will just provide you with a list of all the good qualifying questions and I would love to do so if that were practicable. The characteristics of good prospects, however, are often peculiar to specific industries as well as the product or service being sold. Further, I'm not inclined to fill up pages with no-brainers such as, "Run a credit check to verify that a prospect can pay your invoices."

That said, subsequent chapters will provide important considerations for both prospecting and qualification. And, I will leave you with three broad concepts with application for your qualifying efforts.

1. Closing a sale will always be easier if you first are satisfied that a potential client actually needs your product or service.
2. To the extent possible, verify that a prospect has the ability to spend enough money to justify your time.
3. Determine that your product or service offers the client a demonstrable competitive advantage i.e. USP, Unique Selling Proposition.

From their own experience or with guidance from management, sellers can quickly master the tactics necessary for The Law of Qualification. The critical takeaways from this chapter are acceptance of the fact that all prospects are not created equally along with recognition of the need for qualifying potential new customers.

SIX

THE LAW OF ATTRITION

John Smith – okay, not his real name (and not the one of Pocahontas fame either) – was a good friend of mine throughout college at Indiana University and for several years thereafter. He was an incredibly likeable person, probably because he was very sensitive to the needs of those around him. John was also a bright guy who always got good grades.

Unfortunately, like many of my peers, John chose to major in Sociology. (The joke in Bloomington was that the person serving us ice cream at the DQ almost certainly had a Sociology degree.) So, when both of us ultimately moved to Indianapolis, his career opportunities were limited and he ended up getting his real estate license.

John finally landed a position with the corporate division of a national real estate firm. His job there required him to contact the relocation manager inside other Indianapolis businesses and persuade that person to let John's real estate company find housing for new employees being transferred into the market. His compensation and performance evaluation were dependent on his success at landing those opportunities.

Almost immediately, John developed a good working relationship with the Human Resources Director for a major manufacturing company that, in addition to having a large plant in the city, also had their corporate headquarters in Indianapolis. It was the latter which fostered relatively frequent relocation needs along with real estate opportunities for John.

The same qualities which endeared him to his friends ultimately led to John becoming the exclusive real estate agent for the manufacturing company and he took his customer service responsibilities very seriously. His efforts on behalf of corporate transferees went far above and beyond the call of duty.

Besides showing them lots and lots of available homes, John took his new clients on tours that included everything from schools and libraries to grocery stores and nightclubs. He invited the manufacturer's new Indianapolis residents to be his guests at Chamber of Commerce functions and provided them with contact information for area Rotary and Kiwanis Clubs.

In short, John turned his liaison with the manufacturing company into a fulltime job. The Human Resources Director – quite seriously – offered to provide John with office space at corporate headquarters.

And then the unthinkable happened! One evening while having dinner with friends at a local restaurant, I saw John sitting alone at the bar and went over to say hello. He was clearly agitated, refused to look me in the eye and, when I asked what was wrong, he waved me away dismissively.

I understood his depression soon enough. The front page of the following morning's newspaper trumpeted that the manufacturing company – John's only client – had filed for bankruptcy, ceasing all operations immediately. The manufacturer was out of business and, in relatively short order, so was John.

He wouldn't return my calls after that although I left him messages for several weeks. I heard from a mutual friend that John had left Indianapolis and moved back home with his parents in Nebraska. Sadly, I never heard from him again.

Most salespeople will fail to totally master all of The 22 Unbreakable Laws of Selling and the related concepts. Being a bona fide expert in all sales practices is an elite status reserved for perhaps the top one percent of everyone who tries their hand at selling.

Generally speaking, typical good sellers will excel in some areas while developing moderate skill levels for the other parts of the selling process. Their success comes from possessing at least a modicum of talent for all phases of sales.

While The Law of Attrition is, arguably, no more important than the 21 others discussed in this book, failure to give this concept its due will have dire consequences. More than any of the other chapters relating to the development of new business, The Law of Attrition leads to an inescapable imperative.

Prospect or die!! Experienced salespeople know the truth – many currently active clients will suddenly and surprisingly expire, literally or figuratively. The culprit might be a bankruptcy or a merger or perhaps the retirement or actual death of the business owner.

The reason is irrelevant but the result is critical. In some industries, it is not uncommon for thirty percent of customers to disappear from one year to the next. Since neither managers nor sellers will find a thirty percent sales decrease to be acceptable, responsible salespeople must constantly be identifying and developing replacement clients. Failure to do so (and with apologies to author Arthur Miller) will surely produce the "Death of a Salesman".

I don't mean to sensationalize this topic but, from personal experience, I can testify to the drama associated with the demise of a key account. It's painful – bruising not only to the pocketbook but to the ego as well. Worries about the financial consequences are compounded by feelings of frustration and helplessness. And, of course, job security is another consideration.

My personal solution to the battle with attrition was to borrow an axiom from sports – "the best defense is a good offense". I convinced myself that the loss of my best customers was imminent and I let that fear drive me into a panic prospecting mode. The results from this new mindset were delightful.

First, I began each morning grateful for the business I retained from the previous day. Second, my relentless prospecting produced exponential growth in my active account list. And third, the occasional loss of a good customer didn't affect my 'game' because it had been anticipated.

You may adopt or reject the mind games I played with myself – that's your choice. But, being mentally prepared for inevitable attrition is not optional. You WILL lose existing clients and, typically, it will be through no fault of your own. But the potential devastation is avoided when regular new business prospecting is part of your regimen.

My story about John Smith is, admittedly, an extreme example. Salespeople of only above average intelligence – those smart enough to buy this book, for instance, - would never leave themselves exposed to the vulnerability of having only one client. However, in another respect, John's case is not at all unusual.

All salespeople are different and, consequently, they will each develop certain skill sets more readily than others. Some sellers will enjoy negotiation while others avoid confrontation but provide superior service after the sale. These unique characteristics are natural and entirely acceptable.

It is also predictable that each salesperson will gravitate toward opportunities that best utilize his or her innate talents. So far, so good.

These natural tendencies only become problematical when they are practiced to the exclusion of less comfortable but more appropriate sales processes. A seller, for instance, cannot avoid negotiation by offering a product or service too cheaply. A salesperson must, instead, develop competency in weak areas by repeatedly engaging in a suspect process.

This note of caution applies, of course, to all The 22 Unbreakable Laws of Selling. But, it would be particularly easy to think about attrition only when it actually happens and then to view an account loss as unnatural and unfair.

The Law of Attrition is included in my book because it is inevitable and potentially crippling to a sales career unless it is anticipated and dealt with proactively. Failure to do so will have the unfortunate result of producing seller attrition.

SEVEN

THE LAW OF DECISION MAKERS

"I have three new pieces of business which should close this week," Gene announced, smiling broadly. The small liquor distributorship started each Monday morning with brief activity reports from all of its sales representatives and Gene was the last seller to deliver his pendings.

The promise of three new accounts was the best at the table and normally would have earned Gene positive recognition from his Sales Manager. Instead, his boss wrapped up the meeting and then, rather ominously, asked Gene to join him in the executive's office.

"Gene," the Sales Manager began, "You've been promising to deliver the same three accounts for more than a month and, based on your pending reports, I included the additional revenue in my projections for the owner. Now, both of us want to know why you haven't turned in contracts for this new business. What's the story?"

"Sorry boss," Gene quipped, "But there's really no need to worry. They all loved my presentations and they're just trying to find time to run some numbers before signing our contract."

Gene's assurances notwithstanding, the Sales Manager was still concerned and, with pressure coming from his boss, he was determined to investigate further. "That's good Gene," he said, "But maybe I can help you speed up the process. Please arrange an appointment for both of us to go see the first account on your pending list."

Gene later confirmed a meeting with the target account, a giant liquor store located in an upscale strip mall. "We're all set for Friday morning, boss. We'll be seeing the owner – Bob Smith."

Gene's superior had earned his Sales Manager stripes by first being an excellent seller and, in preparation for the client appointment, he did his customary research. That process included reviewing online information about the prospect available from the state liquor board's web site.

Gene made the introductions to initiate the Friday morning appointment. After a few minutes of perfunctory pleasantries, his boss turned the conversation to serious business.

"So Bob," the Sales Manager began, "Who is Franklin Smith? I noticed that the liquor license for your store is in his name."

At this question, Gene's jaw dropped open as he stared at his boss. Fortunately, Bob didn't appear to notice.

"Oh yes," Bob said. "Franklin is my father. He put up the money to buy the store and, technically speaking, he is the actual owner."

"I see," the Sales Manager responded calmly. "And, does Franklin work here at all?"

"Pretty much whenever he wants," Bob said, starting to laugh. "He comes in often enough to maintain a tight grip on the purse strings."

"Gotcha," the Sales Manager smiled, laughing politely. "Hey, Gene and I would love to meet Franklin, too. Do you think you could set up a time when all four of us can get together?"

"Sure, I'd be happy to," Bob replied. "You'll need to meet him if we're actually going to do some business together."

Gene had remained mum throughout the dialogue between his boss and his prospect, stunned by the revelation of a new decision maker. He barely recovered in time to shake Bob's hand and thank him for his time. Gene walked slowly out of the liquor store, not in a hurry to get to the car and hear the criticism he expected to receive from his boss.

Fortunately, this story had a happy ending. Gene and his Sales Manager were finally able to get an appointment with Franklin Smith (the **real** owner) and, after several meetings, the liquor store started carrying the brands distributed by Gene's company. The decision to do so, of course, was made by father Franklin.

The ending was "happy" in the sense that a deal eventually got done. But, that cheerful conclusion must be tempered with recognition that an agreement could have been reached much sooner had Gene correctly identified the real decision maker from the start.

Instead, Gene wasted precious time trying to sell someone who lacked the authority to buy. If readers will once again reference The Law of Organization or The Law of Numbers, they will quickly appreciate the cost of delay. Top sellers understand that time really is money!

Our hapless friend Gene was, indeed, fortunate to have the guidance of a savvy Sales Manager who recognized the warning signs. Based largely on his personal experience, the boss knew that when deals, apparently pending, don't move forward, there is likely an underlying problem.

Hidden objections or just a seller's poor closing technique can stand in the way of potential contracts. But, failure to negotiate with the actual decision maker is a perhaps surprisingly frequent challenge to getting the business from a prospect.

Not all sales representatives will be lucky enough to have a manager with the focus or insight to guide them through the decision maker minefield. So, motivated sellers must shoulder the responsibility for keeping The Law of Decision Makers top-of-mind, taking care to be absolutely certain to focus their selling attention on the right person.

Top flight salespeople will always conduct at least some preliminary research (see The Law of Preparation) prior to meeting a prospective client. Where appropriate, government agency records, typically available online, can be useful as was the case in this chapter's opening story. A customer's own web site is often a good resource and may include an internal personnel hierarchy that reveals the names of decision makers.

As often as not, however, titles can be misleading. A Brand Manager, for example, may only have responsibility for external marketing. A company's Purchasing Agent can turn out to be a clerical person who simply pays invoices that were approved by someone else. Sellers, then, must be prepared to ask straightforward questions. "I represent Company X. Are you the person who decides whether to buy my product/service?"

Sometimes even this direct approach isn't good enough when ego-driven human nature rears its head. Trust me on this – an apparent decision maker who actually lacks authority will rarely reveal their inability to say "yes". It's true because people without power enjoy being treated as if they are in control. It's also not unusual for real decision makers to use faux buyers to screen pesky sales people.

So, sellers beware! If your sales process appears to be stalled and you have eliminated all other rational reasons, consider the possibility that your contact just isn't the decision maker.

With the caveat that this approach is not for everyone, some salespeople will be comfortable with the practice I adopted many years into my personal selling curve. Having wasted more man-hours than I care to count trying to close people either unable or unwilling to pull the trigger, I started aiming higher up the food chain.

Once I identified a solid prospect, I immediately tried to contact the account's CEO or President. For me at least, this approach was very effective.

To be sure, my calls to the penthouse office were often redirected to a department manager. But, without exception, I found myself referred to someone with the authority to make a decision. And, I was able to introduce myself to the manager by saying, "Your CEO encouraged me to talk with you about my company."

Moreover, I sometimes actually scored an appointment with a CEO who would, ultimately, give me a personal introduction to the appropriate manager. With that, my sale was virtually assured.

While my tactic was certainly aggressive and perhaps even extreme, my intention in sharing it is simply to underscore the significance of this issue. The likelihood that every salesperson will have this experience is almost a certainty.

Trying to close a non-buyer is frustrating and exhausting. Negotiating with a non-decision maker can only be a lose-lose process. At best, it's a waste of time. At worst, it's deflating and maybe even career threatening.

Being sensitized to the importance of correctly identifying decision makers will help sellers stay vigilant and, as a result, be more efficient.

EIGHT

THE LAW OF GATEKEEPERS

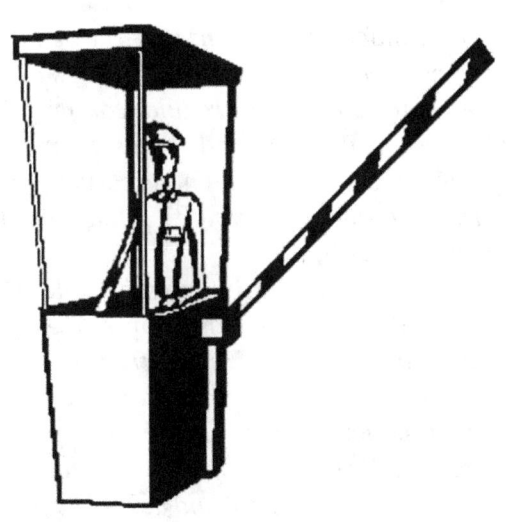

John and Ken had become good friends over the course of working together for several years. They met when, ironically, they were hired on the same day by the corporate division of a national cellular service provider.

The cellular company's corporate entity targeted businesses rather than individuals and had two distinct branches. The first provided customers with internet bandwidth and, as a byproduct, managed the network infrastructure for clients. The second branch primarily sold discounted bundles of cell phone service for multiple employees although, increasingly, VOIP services also fell under this umbrella.

Because the product lines for these two units were both complex and unique, the cellular company employed totally separate sales representatives for each branch. John was hired for the bandwidth/network side while Ken became a seller for cellular phone service.

This structure made perfect sense for the cellular provider. It did produce, however, one somewhat odd result. As often as not, the businesses targeted by the cellular company had a single manager with responsibility for all things technical including both internet connectivity and cell phone service. Consequently, John and Ken were frequently trying to sell different products/services to the same buyer.

Being both good friends and aggressive salesmen, the two regularly compared notes about decision makers they had in common. These shared insights ranged from news about a client's budget to a buyer's favorite restaurant for lunch.

By corporate policy, John and Ken were prevented from combining their products into a joint presentation. Nevertheless, their collaboration was useful and generally produced good results. Generally.....but not always. One account, in particular, was a success story for John and a total bust for Ken.

In this case, the infinite degrees of separation between John and Ken's performance really mattered. The client, headquartered locally, was a multi-national consulting firm with offices all over the world and was, not surprisingly, a huge consumer of all the products and services the two men had to offer.

John had successfully locked up a long-term contract for all of the customer's internet bandwidth and network maintenance worldwide while Ken had nothing to show for his efforts. Worse, word had filtered down through layers of management that the cellular CEO was asking questions about the account.

"Buddy, you've got to help me," Ken pleaded with John as they sipped their after work cocktails. "What am I doing wrong with this client?"

John knew his friend was starting to worry about job security and he was anxious to help. "I don't know, pal. Cynthia is actually one of the nicest buyers I know. I'll tell you what – e-mail your pitch to me and I'll look it over for you."

As usual, Ken followed up right away, sending his proposal from home that night and John reviewed the material in detail. Ken's presentation was extremely well done and John told him so the next morning.

"Your written package just can't be the problem," John reported. "What objections are you getting from Cynthia?"

"None," replied Ken, frowning and shaking his head. "I've never met her! In fact, she won't even return my calls so I'm really shooting in the dark."

"Oh," John nodded. "Now **that's** a problem."

A few nights later, the cellular company held its annual performance recognition dinner and Ken caught up with John at the bar. "Who's your female guest?" Ken asked with a conspiratorial wink.

"Why, that's Beverly," John answered, genuinely surprised. "She's Cynthia's Administrative Assistant – haven't you met her?"

"Oh," Ken sheepishly gulped. "I've talked to her on the phone but I never got her name."

John could have piled on. He could have told Ken that he sent Beverly flowers for her May 18th birthday, that her husband was named Keith and her three year-old daughter was Emily. Instead, John introduced his friend to Beverly who ultimately helped Ken meet Cynthia.

Had he thought about it sooner, John could have told Ken that Beverly was instrumental in connecting him with Cynthia. But it never crossed John's mind because paying attention to and developing a relationship with gatekeepers had become second nature to him.

Without exception, new sellers have this trying experience in their future. All dressed up and no place to go! With a thoughtful, compelling proposal in hand, sales representatives are confounded by their total inability to get through to their prospect for the opportunity to make their presentation.

When rookie salespeople signed on for their new profession, they expected to be faced with objections from their target customers. They knew there would be challenging negotiations over price and demanding service obligations to be met. What they didn't anticipate was that the most vexing hurdle they would face could be simply getting an appointment with their client.

More often than not, just getting a new account on the telephone is a major problem because virtually every manager with real authority relies on some form of gatekeeper. The position might simply be held by the receptionist or it could be someone with a title suggesting they are in control. (See The Law of Decision Makers.) But rest assured that all decision makers have someone screening calls and appointments.

The inability to make any contact with a target account is disheartening (bordering on depressing). And, as failed attempts multiply, the process becomes more and more discouraging. Sadly, many sales representatives vent their growing frustration on the gatekeeper. I've overheard more than one seller saying, "Just tell him I called.....**again**" or "Doesn't she ever return phone calls?"

These emotionally charged comments, of course, ignore that old adage – "Don't shoot the messenger." More to the point, they cast a negative umbrella over the entire communication process, a nuance certain to be passed on from the gatekeeper to the prospective client.

Smart sellers (including those reading this book) will initiate their pursuit of a new prospect with an entirely different mindset. They will assume from the start that a gatekeeper exists, making the correct identification of that person their first priority.

These bright salespeople will understand that the gatekeeper was chosen by their superior and, therefore, has been vested with the trust and confidence of the decision maker. Seasoned sales representatives have probably even witnessed the promotion of gatekeepers to positions of management authority.

As a consequence, good sellers work hard to cultivate positive, independent relationships with key gatekeepers. The karma shared with a gatekeeper almost always gets passed along to the decision maker and certainly opens the door to communication with the superior.

In this chapter's vignette, Ken was, in all other respects, an excellent salesman. However, by ignoring The Law of Gatekeepers, he missed out on getting help from the one person with direct access to his target account. This oversight cost him both time and money and it's a mistake my readers should avoid.

Getting past a gatekeeper won't guarantee making a sale. But, having access blocked by a gatekeeper eliminates all hope of selling!

NINE

THE LAW OF NEEDS

The firm that hired Gary as a sales representative was a large battery distributorship representing all the major brands (Duracell, Energizer, etc.). The company stocked customers (primarily retailers) with all sizes of batteries powering everything from large flashlights to watches and cameras. Besides offering competitive wholesale pricing, the distributor provided clients (at no charge) with an impressive array of display cases and, where appropriate, aisle end caps.

Gary was fresh out of college and a rookie seller in all respects, having just been on staff for a couple of weeks. His company sent all new hires off to sales "camp", an intense, five-day training regimen and Gary was scheduled for that protocol the following week.

Meanwhile, he occupied his time memorizing the distributor's sales brochures, product lines and price schedule. So, except for training and experience, Gary was good to go – at least his Sales Manager thought so when he stopped by Gary's cubicle with a lead.

"Hey rookie," the manager bellowed, loud enough for all the other salespeople to hear. "We got a call this morning from a brand new account. Why don't you make yourself useful and see if you can sell them something!"

"Yes sir," Gary enthused, stopping just short of saluting. Understandably, he was bored with just sitting around the office and, like most new sellers, he was chomping at the bit, ready for action. He was also, of course, too green to know what he didn't know.

The pink message slip his boss left him was from Betty Worth at Freshness Bakeries. Gary was certainly familiar with the Freshness brand – the business had more than twenty different locations in the market plus their products were also sold by several of the local grocery store chains. It crossed his mind that expanding into the sale of batteries seemed rather odd for a bakery but, since the lead was a call-in, Gary quickly decided not to worry about the logic of the prospect.

He called his new "client" back right away and was immediately connected directly to Betty Worth. She thanked Gary for his quick response and the two agreed to meet the following afternoon.

The battery distributor provided excellent support materials for its sales staff which included not only sample product packets but cardboard cutouts of display cases as well. Every seller was equipped with a laptop, pre-loaded with presentation templates that could be customized for individual company merchandise.

Gary grabbed one of everything from the sales store room, determined to dazzle Freshness Bakeries with his firm's complete product line. He then assembled matching files on his computer and, by Noon the next day, he had created a very slick PowerPoint slide show, the quality of which was exceeded only by its length.

Gary could barely balance all of his presentation materials as he was ushered into his prospect's office but he managed to set everything down, making room for his computer on her desk by carefully moving aside a lovely crystal award for "Betty Worth, Public Relations". He was almost out of breath but managed to gush, "Thank you for your call Ms. Worth. It's really nice to meet you."

"It's good to see you as well, Gary, and please call me Betty," she replied, talking to him but surveying all the items Gary had brought with a somewhat mystified expression. "I'm wondering if…..," she began but stopped mid-sentence when Gary raised his hand.

"I know you'll have lots of questions," he interrupted. He didn't intend to be rude but the adrenaline rush of his first sales call made him overly aggressive. "And I'm here to answer all of them but please let me introduce you to our company first."

Overwhelmed (and perhaps mildly amused) by the force of Gary's enthusiasm, Betty simply nodded her assent. With that, he launched his slide show, providing carefully scripted *commentary for each changing screen. Along the way, he erected cardboard displays and positioned battery samples in front of Betty as she sat at her desk. Leaving no facet of his company's business untouched, Gary's presentation lasted nearly two hours.*

When Gary's silence indicated the show was finally over, Betty politely thanked him for his work. "But Freshness is in the bakery business," she continued, "and we really don't have any interest in selling batteries."

Before Gary could give voice to the crestfallen expression on his face, Betty went on to explain why she had called the battery distributor. "This year, Freshness Bakeries will be supporting the local Toys for Tots campaign with the purchase of several thousand gifts for children. We just learned from the charity that the families of the kids who benefit often can't even afford the batteries needed for the toys. So, we were hoping your company might partner with us and Toys for Tots."

"I would have told you that," she added, "if you had only asked."

Intentionally or otherwise, Betty really hit the nail on the head. The negative consequences of this story – both embarrassing and a colossal waste of time – could have been avoided by asking questions…..first!

Readers may think my vignette is somewhat extreme – surely business communication is rarely this bad. But, to the contrary, this scenario plays itself out with frightening frequency and will, in fact, occur almost inevitably every time a salesperson decides to talk first and listen later.

The correct sequence in the selling process demands that salespeople begin by asking questions…..lots of questions. This procedure, in sales parlance, is known as a Client Needs Analysis (CNA) and it should, without exception, be conducted during the first contact with a prospective customer.

The tendency for sellers, both new and experienced, is to give the CNA mostly lip service. They are, understandably, anxious to move the sales process forward, having properly qualified a potential client, identified the decision maker and gotten past the gatekeeper for the initial contact. Simply stated, salespeople often view using the first meeting with a prospect to simply ask questions as a waste of time.

Successful sellers, however, discipline themselves to always initiate a customer relationship with a Client Needs Analysis. They have learned – often the hard way – that this practice helps them avoid the frustration of trying to pound a square peg into a round hole. They know they must conduct a CNA in order to focus their sales presentation on the products/services that a prospect both wants and needs.

Your Sales Managers should be able to provide you with a Client Needs Analysis questionnaire customized for your industry. But, a short list of sample questions will help me illustrate the critical point.

- History of the prospect's business
- A profile of both existing and potential customers
- Primary competitors
- USP (Unique Selling Proposition)
- Best selling products/services
- Price points/margins

In a vacuum, the sales presentation you would generate for a potential new client would necessarily be of the one-size-fits-all variety. Now consider, armed with answers to these questions, how much more tailored your sales pitch would become.

Given the choice, I would prefer trying to hit the bulls eye with a rifle rather than a shotgun. Metaphorically speaking, the Client Needs Analysis becomes the scope mounted on the rifle – a good CNA helps focus on the target.

So, the Client Needs Analysis accomplishes the very real and necessary task of identifying which of the seller's products/services is the best fit for the customer. But, the CNA protocol delivers at least two significant ancillary benefits as well.

First, conducting a Client Needs Analysis positions a seller as a legitimate business partner for the prospect. No one likes to think of themselves as being "sold" and the CNA questioning process helps a customer perceive a salesperson as a problem-solver rather than simply a peddler.

Second, a properly executed Client Needs Analysis forces a customer to talk.....a lot! Note this maxim of human nature – people love to talk about themselves and they love those (you) who facilitate that talking!

On an imaginary timeline, it seemed to make sense for The Law of Needs to follow qualifications, decision makers and gatekeepers. However, if the chapters of this book were ordered purely by importance, this would likely be #1. That said, I'll conclude this chapter with a few quick tips on the actual process of conducting a Client Needs Analysis.

- Take copious notes and do so without fear that clients will be insulted because a seller is writing while they are talking. In truth, customers are flattered when salespeople think their words are that important.
- For much the same reason, don't rush a CNA meeting. The process should continue for as long as the prospect keeps talking.
- Remember that the seller's role during a client needs analysis procedure is to <u>ask</u> questions, not answer them.

TEN

THE LAW OF PRESENTATIONS

Bryan had just graduated from college with dual majors in Marketing and Psychology. His grades were excellent, he had already been accepted for admission to his school's combined MBA/JD program and his parents were both willing and able to fund his continuing education. So, other than being understandably somewhat classroom weary, Bryan was prepared to follow his charted career path. Except that.....

The year was 2002 and the real estate market was sizzling with prices increasing by twenty percent or more every year. Several of Bryan's good friends were already selling real estate and appeared to be getting rich. A couple of the top nationally branded real estate firms actively recruited sellers on campus and one of them made Bryan an offer he was unable to refuse. And, so it was that his academic pursuits ended and his life in sales began.

Bryan signed on with a large franchisee affiliated with Century 21 Real Estate and he was busy even before the ink was dry on his new business cards. Century 21 had a well deserved good reputation for providing its professionals with award-winning training and coaching but, in the over-heated real estate environment, there was little time to complete the lessons. Like most of his peers, Bryan chose to put training on the back burner and he was seeing potential clients shortly after settling into his assigned cubicle.

The good news was that there was no shortage of homeowners looking to cash out of houses they had owned for only a few years or, in some cases, for only a few months. The other news was that these would-be home sellers had the luxury of being very selective when choosing between eager real estate agents. As a consequence, it was common for homeowners to interview several agents before deciding on a representative.

Bryan received just such a call from Joe and Missy Franklin and made an appointment to meet the couple at their home. In preparation for what he understood would be a screening interview, Bryan assembled a collection of promotional pages from the wall of sales material available in the Century 21 office. Included in his packet was a Client Needs Analysis questionnaire which he used to structure his conversation with the Franklins.

Bryan's meeting with the couple seemed to go quite well. Joe and Missy responded expansively to his prepared questions and the interview lasted nearly three hours during which they shared a great deal of information about their motivation for selling their home. Bryan returned to his office brimming with confidence that his new "friends" would soon become new "clients". At the conclusion of their time together, the Franklins asked Bryan to prepare a written proposal for review, a request he regarded as a certain buying signal.

Anxious to get his new deal under contract, Bryan located the standard representation agreement on the Century 21 hard drive and immediately e-mailed the document to the Franklins. The text of his e-mail was simple and straightforward – "I enjoyed meeting both of you. Please sign and return the attached contract so we can start working together."

When he checked his e-mail inbox the following day, Bryan was surprised to find nothing from the Franklin couple. He tried reaching them by phone but could only leave them a voicemail. This sequence was repeated for several days. Finally, nearly a week later, Bryan received an e-mail reply, also simple and straightforward – "We have signed with an agent from RE/MAX. Thank you for your submission. Joe and Missy Franklin."

Given the poor results from his efforts, it would be easy to not even give our friend Bryan credit for trying. But, awarding him the proverbial goose egg would ignore the fact that Bryan actually did some things correctly.

For instance, he properly identified the decision makers and successfully secured a face-to-face meeting with them. And, he used that initial appointment to conduct a thorough Client Needs Analysis. Further, he did (albeit unsuccessfully) attempt a feeble close by asking for the business in his e-mail to the potential clients. In between, however, he completely whiffed on a most critical step in the selling process described here as The Law of Presentations.

The creation and execution of effective presentations requires an understanding of elements that are both substantive and subtle, cognitive and subliminal. In an effort to simplify this seemingly complex subject, I decided to rely on the time-tested method of who, what, where, when and why.

Who. To avoid wasting precious time (and to insure proper emphasis on a seller's most salient points), the presentation must be made to the decision maker. To the chapter devoted to this topic, I would only add that there may be multiple decision makers and/or others whose input may significantly impact the final decision. Whenever possible, all of these people should be included in the presentation.

What. If not for my interest in creating brief, snappy titles, this chapter would have been called The Law of Written Presentations. So, trust me when I say that all presentations must be in writing although neither the format (Word, PowerPoint, pdf, etc.) nor the medium (paper, laptop, WebEx, etc.) really matter.

In a perfect world, a seller will always be able to close the sale at the conclusion of the presentation. But, the world isn't perfect and buyers frequently require time to think before making a decision. In those cases, a sales representative needs a written copy (paper, flash drive, e-mail attachment) to leave behind for the prospect to review.

At the risk of putting too fine a point on this written aspect of the "what", superior sellers will give serious consideration to the visual construction of the presentation they write. During both the actual delivery and the subsequent private review, what parts of a presentation will attract the attention of a prospective client? Various theories on this question are beyond the scope of my book but one good rule of thumb is that lots of white space on a page produces better focus on limited written material.

Generally speaking, the contents of a presentation can be divided into three decidedly unequal parts. The first, and by far the largest, portion of the written document should be devoted to a re-statement of the information gathered during the Client Needs Analysis including the prospect's greatest challenges, competitive advantages and specific growth opportunities. Smart sellers will incorporate the client's own words into these descriptions.

The second, and considerably shorter, section of a presentation can be used to extol the virtues of a seller's products/services. Besides being modest in length, these advantages should all be presented within the context of the client's needs i.e. how will a relationship between the seller and buyer enhance the prospect's business.

Finally, a presentation should conclude with the fiscal details of the proposed sales agreement including quantity, price and any added value elements. As a matter of style, it's critical that even these seemingly dry numbers be presented as a solution to the client's needs and the associated costs described as an investment.

The initial draft of a written presentation should be carefully reviewed for what is best thought of as internal logic. The opening statements of client needs should couple naturally with the description of seller capabilities, leading logically to the proposed solution. When these three elements fit tightly as hand in glove, the "what" becomes a genuinely compelling presentation.

Where. Presentations are best delivered face-to-face and I would strongly encourage managers to facilitate this protocol even when it requires the additional expense of travel and lodging. Being in the same room with their clients makes sales representatives considerably more effective. Besides gaining the ability to actually shake hands, sellers can adjust presentations mid-course, reacting to the nuances of audience body language.

Unfortunately, it is often customers who are reluctant to make time for in-person appointments. But, fortunately, our digital world has created alternatives such as Go-To-Meetings and WebEx. While these are not ideal substitutes for face-to-face meetings, they are acceptable (and necessary) opportunities to collect feedback while making presentations.

Buyers will sometimes ask sellers to simply send a proposal via e-mail or to drop the document in the mail. Throughout my sales career, I have consistently said "No" to these requests and I encourage my readers to do the same. Decision makers have typically respected my insistence on a reasonable opportunity to make my presentation and those that didn't weren't really interested in doing business with me.

When. It may seem simplistic to suggest that a presentation should be made when a prospect is ready to make a purchase but timing occasionally deserves more consideration. I mentioned earlier that the ideal conclusion to a presentation is walking away with an order, an unlikely result when a prospect is just gathering information for a possible purchase. Savvy sellers will probe potential clients on this issue, maintaining dialogue but delaying a full blown presentation for the right time.

Some customers, as part of their buying process, will conduct "cattle calls", lining up appointments with multiple sellers and scheduling the meetings back-to-back-to-back. Pretty obviously, a sales representative stuck with the first meeting has little chance of closing a sale. In this case, having a good relationship with the decision maker's "gate keeper" can help a seller secure the final appointment when a real decision might be made.

Why. When constructed as I have described, the written presentation becomes a seamless, logically compelling argument which leads to an inescapable conclusion – it only makes good sense for the potential customer to purchase a seller's products/services. As such, the presentation should be a sales representative's best tool for closing a piece of business.

Beyond serving as a critical aid to closing the deal, there are other reasons, equally as important, why skillful delivery of a written presentation makes a difference. These are best appreciated when sellers adjust the context to take a somewhat broader view of the presentation appointment with a potential customer. Besides just being the chance to make a sale, this meeting provides a sales representative with the opportunity to build a strong client relationship from which multiple sales will flow in the future.

Attainment of that relationship goal relies heavily on successful execution of the first portion of the written presentation – "...re-statement of the information gathered during the Client Needs Analysis..." Consider the ancillary benefits that accrue from this process.

Recitation of facts learned during the CNA demonstrates that the seller was listening (paying attention) when the customer was talking. Descriptions of the prospect's business will seem particularly insightful since they use the client's own words! Both of these resulting perceptions build trust and respect, key ingredients in the foundation of a strong business relationship.

I'll bring the importance of this chapter home by returning once more to our buddy Bryan, the real estate agent. During his Client Needs Analysis meeting with Joe and Missy, Bryan learned that the couple would not be able to close on a sale quicker than 120 days (they had no place to go) and that they were unwilling to accept an offer that included any contingencies.

When he e-mailed a contract to Joe and Missy, Bryan totally failed to acknowledge or address these client concerns, electing to send them a "submission" instead of making a "presentation". Bryan dropped the ball and lost the sale. Please don't make the same mistake.

ELEVEN

THE LAW OF PRACTICE

Jon was a third year law student at Indiana University. In addition to his full-time course load, he also worked thirty hours weekly as law clerk for a local Bloomington attorney named Ted.

Jon both liked and respected the attorney a great deal in spite of the fact that Ted was a stern task master. The lawyer was incredibly bright – Ted was elected Student Body President as an undergraduate at IU (where he was Phi Beta Kappa) and was also President of his class at Harvard Law School. Naturally, Ted went on to become a Judge for the Indiana Court of Appeals. His challenging style wasn't intentional – he simply expected everyone else to be equally intelligent.

Jon's work as a clerk provided important real life experience while law school tended to be more theoretical. IU, like most universities, utilized the Socratic method of teaching the law, a protocol supposedly modeled after Socrates and his pupils. The Greek philosopher would ask his students a question and then would logically challenge their answer, proving that an effective argument was available for any response.

This academic process did have some practical application but neither school nor his clerkship gave Jon actual courtroom training. One course that offered a hint of trial experience required Jon to interview prospective witnesses (law student actors), reviewing their possible testimony. Candidly, Jon did not do well at this exercise. In fact, he performed very poorly and was concerned enough to share the deficiency with Ted.

So, as the third year law school ritual of Moot Court approached, Jon asked Ted to guide his preparation. Performed before an audience of peers, Jon was required to argue a case before a panel of judges (again, law school actors), fielding their questions and defending his position. Moot Court was a terrifying experience for even the most accomplished students.

"The key to your success," Ted began in his typical professorial style, "will be rehearsal." He was wagging his finger in Jon's face, a mannerism that would have appeared rude to anyone that didn't know his good intentions.

"Okay," Jon nodded obediently. "I need to practice."

"Rehearsal, rehearsal, rehearsal," he repeated, louder this time for emphasis.

"Yes sir – got it!" Jon was almost shouting to prove his agreement.

"Good, good," Ted said, rubbing his palms together with relish. "Let's start right now – let me hear your presentation."

Knowing that argument would be futile, Jon pulled his notes from his briefcase and nervously delivered his prepared remarks. To his surprise, Ted let him finish without interruption. Afterward, Ted made only a few constructive suggestions and asked Jon to practice again in front of his mirror at home.

Ted intercepted Jon the moment he arrived at the office the next day and made the student rehearse his presentation again. This time, he interrupted Jon to challenge a legal interpretation which the two discussed at some length. Much to Jon's dismay, the lawyer caught him again just before the office closed for the day, asking his clerk for yet another rehearsal which produced yet another, different interruption and lengthy discussion.

These apparently spontaneous rehearsal requests continued with roughly the same frequency and results for more than a week at which point, counting additional deliveries in the mirror at home, Jon had practiced his presentation nearly twenty times. His final rehearsal for Ted was marked by multiple interruptions from the attorney and Jon, somewhat to his own surprise, handled all of Ted's objections comfortably and confidently.

Unlike many of my chapter-opening vignettes, this story has a happy ending. I'm delighted to report that Jon received a passing grade (it was Pass/Fail) for Moot Court and graduated from law school on schedule, a result made all the more pleasing because – as you may have guessed – this story is about me. And, perhaps because of my legal training, it seemed only apropos to use the practice of law to demonstrate The Law of Practice.

It's such a simple instruction – "Please practice your presentation before your appointment" – and, as a Sales Manager, I never got any argument from my account managers. And yet, after the fact, virtually all of my sellers admitted they had skipped (ignored, forgotten) the rehearsal.

I've never fully understood why so many sales representatives are reluctant to practice – perhaps they just think it's a silly exercise. But, one thing I do know is that account executives who fail to practice are depriving themselves of critical benefits.

Sellers need to appreciate that proof-reading a presentation is not an adequate substitute for verbalizing the same document. The words sound qualitatively different when heard out loud and provide a legitimate opportunity to gauge pace and timing while identifying appropriate places for emphasis.

Practicing in front of a mirror has unique advantages. Typically performed solo, this method of delivery encourages sales representatives to comfortably test the visual effectiveness of hand gestures and facial expressions.

The biggest payoffs come from rehearsals conducted in front of an audience. While friends and family members are acceptable for this exercise (they probably will be very direct with their critiques), sellers will generally collect the most useful feedback from co-workers. Friends will provide significant visual cues (interested or bored, smile or frown, clear or confused) but only peers can actually challenge a presentation on its merits.

Sales representatives must encourage co-workers to interrupt the trial presentation with frequent questions and to play devil's advocate with final conclusions and proposals. Their inside knowledge of the seller's business makes their feedback particularly meaningful.

When taken together, the practice benefits I have described give sellers the chance to smooth out their delivery (both verbally and physically) and to identify – and fix – errors in syntax, logic and fact. Absent these rehearsals, mistakes or weaknesses in a presentation will be exposed in front of a prospective client.

I should point out that practicing has application for other phases of the selling process including the Client Needs Analysis and all different closing techniques. But, for my money, it is the presentation where rehearsal is of paramount importance.

There is much truth to that old cliché – "If you fail to practice, you practice to fail." Is it worth the extra time and effort to know you are fully prepared for every significant contact you have with a prospective client? If "yes" is your answer, you know what must be done.

Practice, practice, practice!

TWELVE

THE LAW OF EARS

Susan and Joel met in college and married shortly after graduation. Still happily wedded after eight years, they were blessed with two children. Susan was a stay-at-home mom who enjoyed visiting antique shops when she could break away. Joel was a rising young executive and managed to play golf most weekends. They shared an account with ancestry.com and worked together on their family tree one or two evenings a month.

Supported by Joel's success, they had just moved into a new home – a larger house in a more up-scale neighborhood. Only days after they finished unpacking, Susan and Joel were invited to a BBQ Block Party hosted by one of their neighbors. Excited by the opportunity to make new friends, they hired a sitter for the evening and walked to the event a few doors down the street.

Consistent with their plan, the couple quickly separated at the party in an effort to meet more people. They occasionally waved at each other across the lawn and they crossed paths periodically but they really didn't spend any time together until they walked back home. Once there, they decided to have a nightcap and compare notes.

"I'll go first," Susan gushed. "I talked with many really nice people but the most interesting person I met was a fellow named Richard!"

"No kidding," Joel interrupted, starting to smile. "That's funny."

"I'm serious," Susan protested. "We have so much in common that we talked for quite awhile. It turns out that Richard is very interested in both antiques and genealogy. You've really got to meet him!"

"Calm down, Honey," Joel said soothingly. "I did meet Richard and I'm only laughing because he was also my favorite person at the party. He follows the PGA Tour and we talked about golf forever."

"Oh, that's wonderful," Susan said, clearly relieved that Joel shared her opinion. "By the way, what does Richard do for a living?"

"Gee, I really don't know," Joel replied, somewhat surprised to realize he didn't know the answer. "But, I'll find out when I call him to schedule a round of golf."

I can hear you now. "That's a nice little story, Jon, but what the heck does it have to do with sales?" Well, to the extent that a warm relationship can help close a deal – and I contend it is often critical – my vignette has everything to do with sales.

Now it's my turn to ask you a couple of questions. First, have you ever met someone that you liked instantly and were anxious to see again? That's the easy one – of course you have – we all have. My second, and more challenging, question is whether you can accurately rewind the first conversation you had with that person and, in doing so, isolate the reason(s) you liked him/her so much?

Your memory of that initial dialogue is likely flawed and here's why. You will logically assume that your positive impression of a new acquaintance results from that person being really interesting or entertaining or intelligent. Sometimes that's true. But, more often, we are attracted to people who are interested in us, who make us feel witty or bright. We don't like them because of what they say. Rather, we like them because they listen to us.

The significance of this lesson will probably be better appreciated if I reveal more about the first meetings between Susan, Joel and Richard – the rest of the story, as it were.

- Richard inherited a tea set from his mother's aunt and that was the closest thing to an antique in his household.
- Besides seeing pictures and hearing anecdotes about his great-grandparents, Richard knew nothing about his own family tree.

- Richard typically played golf once a year at his company's annual outing. He did, however, read the Sports section in the daily newspaper.
- Neither Susan nor Joel knew what Richard did for a living because he never talked about himself.
- Richard was a life insurance salesman, one of the most brutal selling professions on the planet. Susan and Joel subsequently became clients.

Richard didn't mislead the couple – he was genuinely interested in everyone he met. That said, Richard had certainly learned that showing interest in others provided the foundation for positive relationships and he trained himself to become a really good listener.

You have, no doubt, heard someone say, "She would be a great salesperson because she has the gift of gab." (You may, in fact, have uttered these words yourself.) But this chapter should turn that old supposed axiom on its ear (pun intended).

Sellers will demonstrably improve the results of their work by remembering and practicing three simple rules.

1. People like to do business with people they like;
2. There is nothing people enjoy more than talking about themselves; and,
3. Ipso facto, get people to talk about themselves and they will like you.

To be sure, there are other reasons to be a good listener – chief among them being the ability to hear nuances from a prospect that will sharpen a sales pitch. (Refer again to The Law of Needs.) But, that single opportunity to make a good first impression remains the paramount reason for understanding The Law of Ears.

Because so much of this chapter seems comfortably intuitive, I feel compelled to close with an important caveat. Contrary to what you may think, being a good listener DOES NOT come naturally.

Please re-read rule #2 above. This rule doesn't apply only to your prospective customers – it also applies to you! Human nature is such that we would rather talk than listen.

Developing the ability to use the ears before the mouth is an art form that requires exquisite discipline. Becoming a master of this practice will give sellers a distinct advantage over their competition.

THIRTEEN

THE LAW OF ATTENTION

Jerry was the newest addition to the sales team and everyone in the company was excited about his potential. He had interviewed with the Director of Sales, the General Sales Manager and the VP of Human Resources and all three of these senior staff members were convinced that Jerry could be a great salesperson.

When they met to discuss his candidacy, their observations were very similar. They agreed that Jerry was most impressive in his articulation of the sequential steps in the sales process and his description of how he, if hired, would effectively execute each protocol. In fact, the managers conceded, his responses to their questions were so detailed and thorough that there was little left to ask when Jerry finished talking. He was, so it seemed, a lock to become a top seller for the organization.

Jerry was hired in short order and turned out to be, in many respects a model employee. He was a quick learner, a hard worker and he kept his managers abreast of his daily activities. It was this latter trait, however, that began to wear on the senior staff – proof positive that it's possible to have too much of a good thing.

Jerry didn't let any of his activities pass – phone calls, letters, e-mails, appointments – without describing the event to his manager in excruciating detail. To his boss, it seemed as if every time he looked up from his desk, Jerry was standing in the doorway, waiting for permission to enter.

And, the rookie seller practiced equal opportunity when it came to sharing his news. When his direct manager was unavailable, he would track down the Director of Sales and describe his latest activity. Sometimes, Jerry would even interrupt the HR manager with whom he had interviewed, telling his story to someone who actually knew little about sales.

It's not that the senior staff wasn't interested in what Jerry was doing. They were, of course, pleased that he was working so hard. But they, too, were busy and they generally were interrupted by sellers only to solve problems.

Without even realizing they were doing so, managers began to avoid conversations with Jerry. If they ran into him in a hallway, they might duck into the restroom. If they saw him headed for their office, they would sometimes pick up the phone and pretend to be deep in conversation. When he was seated across the desk, they would shuffle through papers or review message slips, rarely looking Jerry in the eye.

The new sales guy was equally as verbose during sales meetings. Jerry frequently used those gatherings to share his work stories with his peers, oblivious to the fact that the other sellers were rolling their eyes behind his back. It didn't help that his detailed discourses caused the sales meetings to run over.

To a person, Jerry's managers agreed that the seller talked too often and too much. They would have, however, overlooked their growing frustration with him if Jerry's methods had delivered outstanding results. But, to the contrary, both Sales Managers began receiving complaints from existing and prospective clients.

"He's a really bright, really nice guy," they would say. "But he just doesn't know when to shut up!" Sadly, Jerry was terminated after only a few months on the job.

In my first draft, this chapter was titled, "The Law of Eyes." However, when I saw a chapter about "ears" followed by one focused on "eyes", I found myself thinking the next two chapters should be "nose" and "throat." At that point, I decided to dispense with any more body part titles.

That said, this chapter is primarily concerned with the art of paying attention and most of the necessary observations are made with the eyes. True enough, the ears can detect subtle nuances from speech but the emphasis here is on body activity or language.

"Through the Wormhole with Morgan Freemen" was a series carried by the Science Channel in the summer of 2012. (Yes, I'm a science junkie in my spare time.) Of particular relevance for this chapter was an episode called "Mysteries of the Subconscious" which detailed numerous studies illustrating unintended, unknowing body language demonstrated by most humans.

To say it's important that sellers learn to recognize and correctly interpret these gestures is an understatement. Because a prospect's body language is inadvertent – that is, subconscious – it provides feedback that the client won't/can't verbalize and is, therefore, likely more revealing than anything the customer might say. So, it's not enough for salespeople to be good listeners. They must also have the ability to <u>watch</u> what their clients are saying!

Our hapless friend Jerry was the poster child for the salesman cursed with "the gift of gab." (In fairness, his managers must accept some blame for not recognizing and addressing this malady early in his employment.) Jerry believed he could chat his way through any challenge but ended up talking his way out of a sales career.

All the negative body language was there if only Jerry had been paying attention but he was, unfortunately, oblivious to the signs. Because I identified them for you, it was easy to spot the warning signals in Jerry's story but many seasoned sellers are equally as blind.

It's worth noting here that there is something of a dichotomy in The Law of Attention. The bulk of this chapter is devoted to <u>paying</u> attention but you should also recognize the significance of <u>getting</u> attention.

At the risk of seeming too cute, it's critical for sellers to pay attention to whether they are getting attention, an issue of paramount importance when delivering a client presentation. Through keen observation, accomplished salespeople will notice if they are starting to 'lose the room' and will be prepared to adjust their material as necessary.

If you needed a reason to re-read The Law of Practice, then The Law of Attention can be your excuse. Once a salesperson becomes adept at recognizing and interpreting body language, the value of practice goes up exponentially. The goal of rehearsal is to replicate the feedback a seller is likely to receive from a prospective customer. For that reason, practicing a presentation in front of multiple audiences improves the chances that the account executive will collect the full range of possible responses.

Earlier, I referred to the "art" of paying attention and, when this law is professionally mastered, it deserves that lofty description. Like many of the laws in this book, this one seems intuitive – of course you pay attention to your surroundings!

But, there is a huge difference between the general awareness that all humans possess and the ability to purposefully scrutinize faces and body movements for more subtle feedback. The latter requires not only conscious effort but the added knack for correctly interpreting perceived signals, a talent that generally comes only from experience. That's art!

The challenge presented by The Law of Attention is compounded by yet another requirement. Accomplished sellers must not only recognize and properly read body language – they must also be prepared to alter their own behavior based on the feedback they receive. Consider whether, even if he had recognized his penchant for talking too much, Jerry would have been willing or able to dial it back to an acceptable level?

So, are you going to be Jerry or are you going to be the best salesperson on the planet? Hello?! Are you paying attention?

FOURTEEN

THE LAW OF PERSISTENCE

Before being turned loose on real customers, Tom had to complete his new employer's full week, off-site sales training course. During that intense protocol, he was introduced to the full product mix he would be selling, his company's USP's (Unique Selling Propositions) as well as winning responses to common client objections. Once he finished this orientation instruction, Tom felt he was ready to conquer the world.

On his first day in the office, he was given his monthly quotas for a variety of categories. Like all of the company's sellers, Tom was expected to maintain a strict pricing structure, to increase revenue from established customers and to develop new business.

Generally, his first six months on the job were very successful as Tom consistently met or exceeded his overall revenue goals, a feat accomplished primarily through up-selling existing clients. His Sales Manager received great feedback on Tom from significant, long-standing customers who backed up their positive comments with larger purchase contracts.

However, Tom's success with increasing current business tended to mask a shortcoming in adding new business, a weakness ultimately revealed when he failed to meet his quarterly budget for first-time customers. This deficiency wasn't for lack of effort – Tom's call sheets showed he was making contact with a good number of prospects, all of whom seemed well qualified for revenue potential. He just appeared unable to get prospective clients to commit to his company.

Fortunately for Tom, his otherwise outstanding performance with solid customers made him far too valuable to be severely disciplined for his new business weakness. That said, his Sales Manager was determined to correct the problem even though, when asked, Tom was unable to offer a helpful explanation. Absent meaningful guidance from his employee, the Sales Manager decided to accompany Tom on some appointments with prospects the seller had already seen.

In virtually every case, his supervisor noted, Tom had met with each prospective client twice before. Much to their mutual surprise – Tom the more so – meeting after meeting resulted in good progress including several signed contracts.

"Maybe it's third time charmed," the Sales Manager quipped.

"I guess I need to call on potential new customers more than just a couple of times," Tom concluded, still scratching his head.

It's easy for sellers to become discouraged by the results from the first couple of meetings with new prospects, concluding that further effort would be a waste of time. But, Tom's experience with subsequent appointments suggests that salespeople often throw in the towel too soon.

Rather than losing enthusiasm for potential customers who seem, at best, disinterested early in the sales process, account executives would be better served by recognizing there are many legitimate reasons that explain negative feedback. Timing is a likely culprit.

Target client buyers may simply be too busy to consider a new vendor when they are first approached by a new seller. Or, a buying decision for the salesperson's product/service is not critical at that moment.

More often than not, priming a new business prospect just requires patience which, of course, is a trait rarely exhibited by aggressive salespeople. But, like it or not, sellers must accept the fact that it takes time to develop the respect and trust necessary for a strong business relationship.

Those who question the importance of being a patient person need to study the relevant statistics. Doubters will likely be shocked by the story they tell.

Although it can vary somewhat by industry, the reliable average is 5.3 – that is, 5.3 meaningful contacts with a new business prospect are typically required in order to close a sale! Are you surprised? Absent this knowledge, would you have been inclined to give up on a potential customer sooner?

Trusting that committed sellers will incorporate this statistic into their sales regimen, acting on this number may require something of a delicate touch. Specifically, salespeople must balance the need for persistence with avoiding being a pest.

To that end, it probably makes sense to spread out prospect appointment requests over an acceptable period of time. This approach unavoidably means it will take longer to nurture potential new customers and will require – you guessed it – patience on the part of sellers. But, when asked, I'm confident good salespeople will be willing to trade instant gratification for the security of a strong, long-term business relationship.

The numbers don't lie. Multiple contacts are generally required before a prospect can be converted into a new business partner. Equally as reliable is the fact that, regardless of the product or service you choose to sell, your manager will insist that you develop new clients. The combined weight of these truths should provide sufficient impetus for you to master the discipline of persistence (and patience).

FIFTEEN

THE LAW OF 80-20

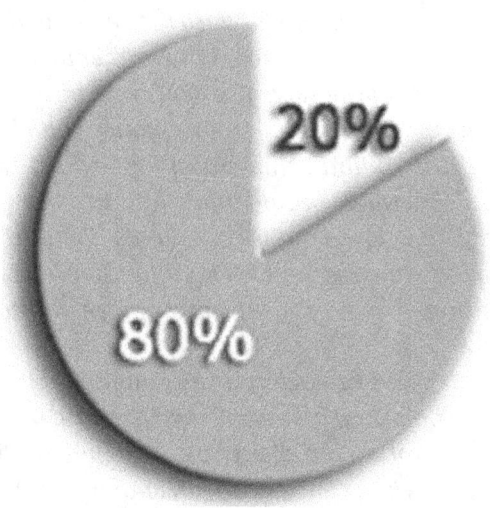

From the time in junior high school when he would lie in bed listening to Top Forty radio, Paul desperately wanted to be a deejay. In high school, he chased his dream by hanging out at his favorite radio station and attending all public promotional events hosted by the disc-jockeys he knew. Shortly after graduation, Paul finally persuaded the Program Director to hire him for a couple of obscure weekend air shifts – Friday and Saturday overnights between two and five o'clock in the morning.

As it happened, Paul showed quite a flair for the job and, within a year, he became a full-time announcer hosting the afternoon drive time slot Monday through Friday. He loved his work including ancillary benefits like backstage passes for all the local concerts plus thousands of adoring (mostly female) fans. The only downside was the pay – he was barely able to make ends meet on his meager salary.

Paul's next few years as a successful deejay were marked by great fun but continued struggles with his personal finances. Not coincidentally, he began to notice that the members of the radio station's sales staff drove much nicer cars and he concluded, correctly, that they must be making more money than he was.

Paul loved the radio business and he decided that moving into the sales department would allow him to continue working in the industry he enjoyed while solving his monetary dilemma. So, he started lobbying his General Manager for a transition into a selling position, a request that his employer granted several months later.

Because Paul was replacing a salesman who had moved to another city, he inherited an established list with approximately seventy-five accounts. This client roster included about fifteen major customers who spent significant money with the station and produced the lion's share of Paul's expected monthly commissions. The remaining sixty or so businesses on the list were a combination of those that were smaller, sporadic advertisers along with some that had never spent money with the station and needed to be developed.

Paul was a smart guy and instantly recognized that the big spenders were the ones that really buttered his bread! Consequently, he immediately set out to blanket these important advertising partners with attention and he made a personal commitment to focus most of his time and energy on these big accounts.

Within a couple of weeks, Paul completed initial introductory meetings with all of his top accounts. To a person, all of these advertisers assured him they were well satisfied with their marketing campaigns on the radio station and each promised to call him with any special needs.

Consistent with his plan, Paul zealously continued to contact his elite accounts, quickly scheduling second appointments with all of them. Paul opened these meetings by telling the ad buyers that he was "just touching base" and again offered to help his clients in any way possible. He repeated this approach for a couple of months until the time arrived for his performance review with his Sales Manager.

Never one to mince words, Paul's boss cut right to the chase with his new seller. "You have been short of your revenue budget for both of your first two months and that's a problem we need to fix."

Oh wow," Paul said, stalling while he tried to catch his breath and collect his thoughts. "I feel like I've been working really hard," he added, knowing this response was insufficient.

"Hard, yes," the manager said quickly, continuing his direct approach. "But, not necessarily smart. The sales reports I'm looking at show that, while the revenue from your top advertisers is steady, you've added virtually no new business from the rest of your accounts."

"Well," Paul said evenly, recovering from his initial loss of balance, "I've definitely devoted the majority of my time to the big spenders on my list because I assumed you would want me to super serve those accounts."

"Yes, those clients are very important," the Sales Manager agreed, transitioning now to a constructive, training mode.

"But, here's the thing – those heavy spenders have already been sold. That business just needs to be maintained which actually takes less time than developing a new advertiser."

"Okay," Paul said slowly, drawing out the word while he tried to digest what he was hearing. "So, just to be clear, you're telling me I should spend less time with my big accounts and more time with my little accounts?"

"Bingo," his boss said, beaming! "That's exactly what I'm saying! And, while you're trying this new approach, here's an added incentive for you to consider. The billing from your top advertisers is just about maxed out and you're still falling short of your goals. The only way for you to achieve your budget is to generate revenue from new customers."

Paul left his performance review intrigued, if not completely sold, by his manager's guidance. And, given his budget shortfalls, Paul knew he had to try something different.

So, he gradually adjusted his time management and, perhaps to his surprise but certainly to his delight, he began hitting his goals in relatively short order. Significantly, his monthly billing increased substantially from <u>both</u> existing and new customers! (Paul's success didn't go unnoticed – two years later he was promoted to Sales Manager.)

To stretch Paul's own metaphor a bit further, he correctly gave his big spenders credit for the butter on his bread but failed to recognize that his smaller accounts put the icing on his cake! But, Paul was fortunate in two ways. First, he was coachable – that is, he was open to learning something new. Second, he was blessed with an experienced and (relatively) patient manager – one who appreciated some of the odd lessons of selling.

Over the years, creative writers have added new and different permutations of the traditional 80-20 rule. But, for purposes of sales in general and this chapter specifically, I'm only going to focus on two:

1. Sellers will realize 80% of their billing from only 20% of their accounts; and,
2. Salespeople should devote 80% of their time with accounts that represent only 20% of their billing.

I'm sure everyone will agree that these two rules seem counter intuitive, particularly the second one. Therefore, the first hurdle for account executives is to ignore logic and accept that both rules have been proven true repeatedly. In some ways, the 80-20 rules really do make sense.

The first rule certainly doesn't require a leap of faith. Even rookie sellers are going to suspect that some accounts are larger than others and seasoned salespeople have the experience to know that the disparity between big and little spenders is quite substantial. If they took the time to do the math, they would find support for the 80-20 split.

The corollary of rule number one is that 80% of a seller's accounts produce only 20% of total billing. Ipso facto, it should take substantially more time to properly service the sheer volume of smaller spending accounts. This conclusion, too, has logical appeal.

Nothing in these 80-20 rules is designed to suggest that salespeople shouldn't give their best attention to their biggest accounts. Without question, sellers must promise their availability to top clients and back it up with prompt, professional service.

But, somewhat ironically, major accounts typically require less hand-holding than their smaller counterparts. Big businesses attract savvy buyers who make confident decisions and generally just call on salespeople to help solve occasional problems. (Note, too, that busy buyers managing large budgets won't appreciate "just touching base" interruptions.) Smaller entrepreneurs, conversely, often rely heavily on account executive expertise in deciding which products/services to purchase.

Over the course of a long career, all salespeople will eventually experience their own versions of the 80-20 rules. By promulgating The Law of 80-20 here, my goal is to help readers get ahead of the curve. By incorporating the 80-20 rules into your time allocations now, your sales will grow exponentially faster.

SIXTEEN

THE LAW OF FLEXIBILITY

As often as not, sales careers begin almost by accident as when a candidate just happens to be in the right place at the right time. But, such was not the case for Barbara who, well before her college graduation, had already made two firm decisions about her life.

First, she wanted to go into selling because she perceived (correctly) a direct correlation between doing good work in sales and earning good money. And, Barbara intended to be very good!

Second, she planned to sell a product that everybody needed. She had concluded (right again) that universal demand would make her sales job easier.

Perhaps because Barbara was always meticulous about remembering and celebrating all of her friends' special occasions, she had noticed that displays of greeting and post cards were truly ubiquitous, showing up everywhere from grocery stores to car washes. After bumping into a swivel rack of mostly food-themed souvenir cards during breakfast at Denny's, Barbara made up her mind and started sending out resumes to area card distributors.

The company that hired Barbara first sent her to their own three day, in-house training seminar. That protocol was very educational for her but, as is the case with many industries, the curriculum focused mostly on introducing new hires to the company's wide product catalog. So, Barbara arrived at work knowing <u>what</u> *she was selling but much less about* <u>how</u> *to sell.*

Her initial week on the job started with a sales meeting conducted in a small auditorium, the only room in the building large enough to accommodate the sixty sellers employed by the company. Barbara's Sales Manager took the microphone and enthusiastically cut to the chase.

"Beneath your seats, you will all find a brochure describing a clever new line of greeting cards we are introducing today," he started, holding up his own copy of the printed piece. "You're going to love these!"

"And," he continued, "You're also going to love our one-day special incentive plan! Are you ready to make some extra cash today?" He used his best carnival barker style.

In unison, the salespeople, including Barbara, roared their approval. Although she hadn't yet heard the deal, Barbara already had visions of dollar signs dancing in her head.

"Okay boys and girls," the Sales Manager smiled, knowing he had the full attention of his people. "It's pretty simple. We're offering a ten percent price discount for every customer who gives us an order for at least two gross of these new greeting cards and we're giving you an extra ten percent commission for every contract! What do you think – can you make this happen?"

Again, the positive response was instant and, again, Barbara joined her excited peers. She was thinking, "How hard can this be?" And, "This is why I got into sales!"

"Now remember folks," the Sales Manager fairly shouted, "This is for today only with a two gross minimum. Now go burn up your phones!"

Even as they applauded, sixty sellers rushed for the auditorium exits. Barbara joined the stampede, anxious to get to her desk and start making calls.

For Barbara, the next eight hours would be, at best, a mixed bag facing, as she did, several immediate challenges. It being her first real day in the office, she hadn't introduced herself to even a single client. Consequently, she had no idea which customers might be good prospects for the special promotion. Further, as a rookie seller for the company, Barbara's account list was made up of mostly small retailers.

Nevertheless, in spite of these obstacles, she did manage to schedule two client appointments for that day. What Barbara may have lacked in sales acumen, she made up for in energy and aggressiveness. She met first with the owner of a single location, 7-Eleven type gasoline and convenience store.

"I really like these new greeting cards," he told Barbara after she had presented the brochure along with her company's one-day special offer. "But, I simply don't need two gross of them – I'll never sell that many. What kind of deal can you give me for a single gross?"

"Well," she said, slightly flummoxed by the question. "Unless you order at least two gross, you'll have to pay our regular wholesale price."

"That's not going to work," he fumed with obvious frustration. "Because they'll pay a lower price, my competitors will be able to sell your cards cheaper than me!"

"I'm really sorry," Barbara replied limply, now experiencing her own frustration. She left the store without making a sale, having likely alienated her first client. Disappointed but not defeated, she moved on to her next appointment, a small gift shop located adjacent to a local tourist attraction.

"These are great cards," the proprietor said, responding to Barbara's presentation. "But two gross is a lot for me to carry in inventory. How about I sign the contract today but only take delivery of a single gross? Then, you can ship and invoice me for the other gross in four months or so?"

"Wow," Barbara stammered, perplexed by another proposed deviation from the company's special offer. And, she was fairly certain a negative response from her would nix this potential sale.

"I'm not sure we can do that," she said, trying to improvise in the only way she knew. "Let me talk with our Sales Manager and I'll call you back later today."

"You do that," the owner replied with a knowing smile.

Unbeknownst to Barbara, the gift shop proprietor and her Sales Manager had known each other for years and the company had often approved special delivery terms for the store owner. By the time she got back to the office, her client had already called her boss, the contract had been written up (under her name) and Barbara ended her first day by (sort of) making a sale.

Barbara's handling of her first two clients was wrong on so many levels that it's hard to know where to begin. Yes, lest you think I'm a man of no compassion, I'm perfectly willing to excuse her transgressions for lack of experience and insufficient guidance from management. Nevertheless, a review of some of Barbara's mistakes will help define The Law of Flexibility.

In their zeal to both follow instructions and to make a sale, many sellers develop tunnel vision, taking a "one size fits all" approach to the proposals they submit to clients. The result is often parallel to trying to squeeze a square peg into a round hole.

To appreciate The Law of Flexibility and to adjust their mentality appropriately for the business of selling, salespeople must accept a simple truth. It is the exception – not the rule – for clients to rubber stamp a presentation exactly as it was written. There will almost always be changes – some minor, some major. So, sellers must always anticipate the need to be flexible.

The process has to begin with a <u>willingness</u> to be flexible. Many salespeople are, by nature, combative, feeling the need to turn customer disagreements into arguments the account executive can "win". I don't require these sellers to change their personalities – I do, however, expect them to exercise the discipline necessary to display flexibility.

As I suggested in The Law of Ears, a top flight salesperson will be a good listener. But, The Law of Flexibility demands that a seller not only listen but also act on a customer's words. The concept of "win-win" can only be achieved when clients are satisfied that they got what they wanted or needed e.g. price, product or terms. Inflexible salespeople leave nothing on the table for prospects to feel good about.

Oddly, the metaphor "quick on your feet" actually means thinking fast and it's a talent flexible sellers need to develop. When client feedback indicates that a sales pitch is going south, salespeople must have the ability to identify the root of the problem on the fly and create an acceptable alternative to get the selling process back on track.

In this context, it's critical to recognize that Barbara's attempt to substitute "check with management" in place of demonstrating immediate flexibility had the potential for disastrous results. Revealing an inability to make required decisions tells customers they are dealing with the wrong person, a weakness from which business relationships may never recover.

Of course, the need for "thinking fast" as well as the riddle of The Law of Flexibility can both be eliminated with intelligent preparation. Smart sellers will approach all significant client discussions with multiple options already in mind. If exceptional contract terms might require prior approval, sharp salespeople will ask management to sign off on them prior to the customer meeting.

These alternate ideas will only be used if they become necessary to close a deal. But, they are ready; sitting comfortably in a salesperson's back pocket.

Boiled down to basics, The Law of Flexibility can be satisfied in two easy steps:

> 1. Know that alternative solutions will probably be required for every successful client presentation and negotiation; and,
> 2. Anticipate customer requests and be prepared with multiple options in advance of prospect appointments.

SEVENTEEN

THE LAW OF NEGOTIATION

It's not as if Brad was absolutely new to sales. He had, after all, spent the past two years selling men's fashions for a national department store chain where he had done well, relatively speaking. But, there were marked differences between that experience and his new job as an account executive for a major tire distributor.

First, retail salespeople enjoy the advantage of having customers come to them. These sellers don't need to worry themselves with prospecting, qualifying and contacting new prospects.

Second, haggling over money isn't part of the retail sales process. All merchandise is affixed with a price tag which defines how much customers must pay.

To his credit, Brad's new Sales Manager reviewed these not so minor distinctions in detail, explaining how they impacted Brad's job description. In particular, as the tire distributor's new seller prepared for his first appointment with an established client, the Sales Manager reminded Brad to open negotiations with an artificially elevated price.

"Kyle is one of those business owners who has to feel like he got the best possible deal," the manager confided. "So, he won't accept your first offer no matter how low it is. Just be ready."

Brad thought he understood the advice from his boss. He made the adjustment to his written proposal and set off to meet with his first client.

"We have the tires you want in stock," Brad told his customer after the two had exchanged some pleasant small talk. "I just need your signature so we can schedule delivery."

"How much is this going to cost me?" Kyle ignored the contract Brad had placed in front of him.

"Your investment will be only $400 per set of four tires," Brad responded, knowing his real bottom line was $300. "How does that sound?"

"It sounds like too much money," Kyle answered, offering no further comment.

"Well, because I really want your business, I would be willing to take $350 per set," Brad said confidently. To him, this negotiation seemed to be going according to script.

"That's still too expensive," Kyle replied matter of factly, his face devoid of emotion.

"Okay, I'll tell you what." Brad knew he was about to fire the last bullet in his gun and the tremor in his voice belied a growing concern. "If you'll sign the order today, I'll accept $300 a set."

"Sorry, I can't afford that much," Kyle said dismissively, standing to indicate the meeting was over.

His Sales Manager showed a wry smile when he heard the story. It turned out that Brad wasn't the first salesman to return empty handed from a meeting with Kyle.

"Sit down, son," the boss said, pointing to a chair. "Let's discuss the art of negotiation."

When viewed in written form, Brad's attempt to negotiate with Kyle appears so lame as to be almost laughable – a conversation I'm sure my readers can't imagine having themselves. But, in some form, this type of ineffective dialogue occurs with surprising frequency and it represents a trap into which even seasoned sellers have fallen. Keep Brad in mind as you review my key rules for successful negotiation.

It takes two to tango. As Brad discovered, trying to negotiate with yourself is a losing proposition. A target client must be seriously, fully engaged in the process for any effort at negotiation to be successful.

The client is not the enemy. At the risk of stating the obvious, it's always important for sellers to have a positive attitude. In the cases of negotiating and closing, however, this can be more challenging because those functions appear to be inherently adversarial. In that competitive construct, it's easy for salespeople to think they are trying to sell something that prospects don't want. This is simply not true – most clients are genuinely interested.

Get a buying commitment. This may be the most salient insight offered in this entire book. Making an offer – any offer – moves a client across a psychological barrier turning a prospect, however reluctant, into a buyer. Consider how the game would have changed if, after his first offer was rejected, Brad had changed the flow of the conversation.

Brad: "Well, what price would you pay?"

Kyle: "I would be willing to pay $200 a set."

Ignoring the amount of his offer, Kyle has now made a buying commitment, the significance of which cannot be overstated. He must now reconcile his action with his mindset and perceive himself as a potential buyer.

At a minimum, Kyle has become engaged in the negotiating process. (Note, too, that the midpoint of Brad's elevated price and Kyle's lowball offer is the target price of $300 for a set of four tires.)

Is it all about the money? Sometimes, it will prove to be virtually impossible to get a prospect involved in the process of negotiating. Rather than press the issue, sellers must learn to recognize when a client's reluctance to meaningfully discuss price results from a different, as yet unidentified, objection. In these cases, talented salespeople will back up, repeat the Client Needs Analysis process, probing for the real issue(s) that need to be addressed.

Always go in high. Always. Experienced sellers know that the negotiating process will, inevitably, require them to make some concessions and following this rule will leave them room to do so.

This proviso has application for other contract issues besides just price. Production schedules, delivery dates and shipping costs are examples of issues that may require negotiation to meet client demands.

Pure wins can be pure losses. Being an aggressive negotiator is generally a good thing but superior salespeople know there are times to take their foot off the gas pedal. All sellers, at some point in their careers, will find they have a client over a barrel because the customer desperately needs their product or service and is willing to pay almost any price.

In such cases, going for the jugular may produce a short-term win but will almost certainly have a long-term cost. The best negotiators work hard to achieve at least the perception of a win-win process and will purposely "leave something on the table" to avoid letting a customer feel like a loser.

Obey all laws. Navigating The Law of Negotiation is made much easier by mastering the rules laid out in the previous chapters of this book. This is particularly true for The Law of Practice and The Law of Presentations. Contrary to what some sellers believe, a skilled negotiator is marked more by technique than style.

To that end, salespeople should identify the likely flow of an upcoming negotiation. This requires deciding on an opening price, anticipating the customer response, protecting a bottom line and preparing for concessions. Role playing (rehearsing) the expected process will always make the actual negotiation smoother and, usually, more fruitful.

Generally, negotiations will occur immediately following a written presentation. In that sequence, the document should demonstrate compelling internal logic which seems to naturally support a fair price.

Create a solid foundation. Prospective clients will always be willing to pay a higher price when they believe in the intrinsic value of the product/service they are buying. But, sellers who try to create that lofty appreciation during negotiations risk having their efforts viewed as simply self-serving.

Salespeople can avoid that frustrating result by pre-selling the virtues of their product/service, well in advance of the negotiating process. In that context, sellers should schedule an entirely separate client appointment to be used only for positive positioning.

EIGHTEEN

THE LAW OF CLOSING

Frederick finished knotting his tie, put on his sports jacket and glanced at his watch. If he were going to complete fifteen face-to-face presentations, as was his goal for the day, he needed to get an early start. It was not yet nine o'clock in the morning when his knock on the door of the first apartment in a sprawling complex was answered by an attractive young couple who, after Frederick introduced himself, invited the salesman inside.

The year was 1967, a time when people still felt entirely comfortable allowing strangers into their homes. And besides, Frederick was obviously a professional holding, as he did, the position of door-to-door sales representative for Britannica Encyclopedias.

In spite of it being only his second week on the job, Frederick was, indeed, very professional. Britannica had immersed him in three intense weeks of training that had actually taught him (go figure) to sell.

During that protocol, Frederick not only learned about his product from A to Z but also participated in repeated role playing exercises. These drills replicated real life scenarios in which the trainees were confronted with every prospect objection imaginable. As a consequence, Frederick's presentations to potential customers were polished by practice and delivered with the confidence that comes from (training) experience.

Once seated in the couple's living room, Frederick introduced his product by handing each of them a volume of the Britannica Encyclopedia, inviting them to open the books and run their hands over the thick glossy pages and admire the many full color pictures. He assured his prospects that the quality of the content matched that of the paper.

Frederick displayed genuine interest in his prospects and, in the course of conversation, learned that both husband and wife were attending college. He innocently asked if they would find the encyclopedia useful in research for required class papers and they both affirmatively replied. (Keep in mind that, at this time, there was no Internet, no Google and no Wikipedia.)

As they continued chatting amiably, the couple's six-month old baby cried out from a spare bedroom. Frederick took the opportunity to let them know that Britannica's encyclopedia program included sending updated replacement volumes on a regular basis. They smiled as he reminded them that, before they knew it, the Britannica product would become a valuable learning tool for their son. Frederick described the Britannica Encyclopedia as an investment in the futures of both the couple and their child.

"That's a good way of looking at it," the husband agreed. "But, if we buy it, do we have to pay for the entire set all at once?"

"Of course not," Frederick replied comfortingly. "Would you prefer to pay monthly or quarterly?"

"I think monthly would be best," the husband answered.

"Good decision," Frederick said, marking a box on the paper he had inconspicuously taken from his briefcase. "That's the way I've filled out the agreement," he added, sliding the contract to the couple who immediately signed the document.

I awoke the next morning horrified that I had committed to spend money I really didn't have. (Oh – did I neglect to mention that I was the male part of the "attractive young couple"?) I quickly called Frederick back and, with a heavy dose of guilt and a sincere apology, I cancelled my order with Britannica Encyclopedias. Nevertheless, even though he didn't end up making a sale, I've always remembered Frederick and his winning style.

It's true – Frederick skipped a critical step in the selling process and ended up wasting his time. He ignored The Law of Qualification and failed to recognize that the couple he targeted didn't meet the financial threshold to be good prospects. But, I'll bet he corrected that oversight because he was certainly smart enough to have mastered The Law of Closing.

I gave serious consideration to combining this chapter with The Law of Negotiation since, more often than not, the two events occur bang-bang. They are, nevertheless, distinct activities with distinct rules.

Negotiating is a process that is sometimes stretched out over hours, days or even weeks. Closing, on the other hand, is a "moment"; that precise time when the success or failure of the preceding sales steps is determined.

Accomplished salespeople are constantly scanning prospect dialogue, on the lookout for "buying signs". These sellers have developed an acute recognition for the subtle signals that clients send when they are vulnerable to being closed.

Not experienced but well trained, Frederick sensed that "moment" when I inquired about payment terms, usually a sure-fire "buying sign". He pounced on my weakness and his instinct was rewarded, at least temporarily, with a sale.

Timing is critical to closing business. As a Sales Manager, I would often accompany a seller for a client presentation, offering constructive criticism after the meeting. Since my role on these occasions was to listen rather than speak, I frequently had to bite my lip as I watched my salesperson first talk a prospect into, and then out of, a contract.

The closing "moment" came and went as my employee droned on according to a prepared script, blissfully oblivious to the missed opportunity. Recognizing "buying signs" from a prospective client isn't brain surgery but, in fairness to my former sellers, it is an acquired talent which generally takes experience to master.

There are a variety of effective closing techniques; more, in fact, than it is feasible for me to condense into a single chapter. (Readers should be able to get a laundry list of these approaches from their respective Sales Managers.) After experimentation, salespeople will typically gravitate to a closing method that best fits their personality and style.

While there isn't a "one size fits all" technique for closing, I do have a personal favorite worthy of serious evaluation by all sellers. In my experience, the "assumptive close" is the easiest to execute and is a successful approach for a high percentage of salespeople.

Fearing rejection ("No"), many sellers struggle with the final step in the sales process. They have completed their written presentation, the prospective customer has no additional questions and the room is suddenly very quiet.

Phrases like "May I have your order please", "Do we have a deal" or "Can you sign this contract" seem stiff and formal and don't easily roll off the tongue. The beauty of the assumptive close lies in avoidance.

In some respects, it is really a phantom or non-event because, with the assumptive close, there is never a time when an account executive directly asks for an order. Instead, the seller circumvents that question by moving on to technical follow-up issues, thereby assuming the client into a contract.

This technique is deceptively easy to execute, primarily because there are so many options from which to choose. Any of the details associated with a contract can provide an "assuming" basis and almost any answer to an assumptive question reinforces a conclusion that the deal is done.

Young Frederick smoothly employed an assumptive close with me when he asked, "Would you prefer to pay monthly or quarterly?" He could have accomplished a similar result with, "Should I deliver your set to you on Friday or would Monday be better?" or "Do you want to pay your first installment by check or credit card?"

You get the idea. If a potential customer responds substantively to this type of question, closing has been achieved assumptively.

Note that the assumptive close is not an effort to "trick" clients into forgetting they haven't approved the sale. To the contrary, it is simply a salesperson moving forward in the belief that a client sees the wisdom in a proposal and, if the seller's presentation was compelling, that assumption will be true!

I'll close this chapter with a lesson that has critical application for both The Law of Negotiation and The Law of Closing. Sometimes, in order to establish a firm bottom line in negotiations or to squeeze a stubborn prospect into saying "yes", a salesperson must be prepared to walk away from business.

I often refer to this as the "take your toys and go home" gambit and it is a surprisingly effective tool. There are some clients – I won't say "many" – who actually enjoy using the ultimate power they wield as buyers to hammer hapless salespeople into submission.

Sellers with the ability to gracefully walk away from the table – "Thank you for your consideration. I hope we can work together next time." – will bring this ugly process to a rapid conclusion. At a minimum, these salespeople will leave a meeting with a measure of self-respect. But, oddly, they will also often leave with a contract in hand because pulling an offer off the table seems to make it more valuable.

Sellers should never view walking away from negotiations as a bluff because their gamble will surely be called. Nevertheless, it's a technique they should consider using <u>before</u> dialogue with a prospect reaches a complete impasse. This is a subtle distinction that account executives will only come to recognize with extensive experience.

Throughout these chapters, I have insisted that practice is required for mastery of the laws in this book and that proviso is of paramount importance with The Law of Closing. For motivation, consider that <u>every</u> step in the selling process – in other words, all your hard work – is designed to move the customer relationship toward closing a sale. If salespeople can't close, they can't sell. Conversely, an accomplished closer can compensate for many other weaknesses.

NINETEEN

THE LAW OF EXPECTATIONS

Our erstwhile friend Paul, the radio advertising salesman to whom you were earlier introduced, was making good progress in his chosen profession. Having become a believer in The Law of 80-20 (see Chapter 15), he was devoting a substantial share of his time to developing new business and doing so with fairly impressive results. But, perceptive readers will not be surprised to hear that Paul still had some painful lessons to learn.

He had just finished going through his written presentation with the owner of a small jewelry store and was anxious to make a sale. The meeting seemed to have gone well and he was confident enough to test the waters with an assumptive close.

"So," Paul said, smiling, "Would you like to begin your radio marketing campaign on Monday or would the following week be better for you?"

"Well," the female owner began noncommittally, "Are you certain the commercial schedule you propose will be a good investment for my small store?"

(Radio is a valuable marketing medium for building top-of-mind brand awareness and, like most advertising vehicles, radio works best when utilized consistently over an extended period of time. Understanding the wisdom of a long-term commitment, Paul's proposal called for the jewelry store to air the same commercial schedule every week for six consecutive months.)

"Oh yes," Paul enthused! He sensed, correctly, that his prospective client would require only a gentle nudge before signing off on the deal. "Advertising on my radio station will definitely make your cash register ring!"

"If you're sure," she said, her inflection indicating this was a question.

"No doubt," Paul answered definitively, adding, "This marketing campaign is a guaranteed winner!"

"Alright then," the owner conceded. "Where do I sign?"

Paul wrote up the advertising contract for the jewelry store, satisfied that his persuasive powers had closed the deal. He was, therefore, blindsided when the business owner called only a week later to cancel her marketing campaign.

"You promised me results," she shouted angrily. "And my sales haven't increased at all this week!"

"It's only been a week," he stammered, struggling to catch his breath. "You have to give advertising time before it has any effect." Paul's explanation was reasonable but he knew how his client was going to respond.

"That's not what you said when you sold me these silly commercials," she hissed. "You gave me your personal guarantee that my cash register would ring and that just hasn't happened. Cancel my order immediately," she concluded, breaking the connection without even saying goodbye.

Both Paul and his radio station would survive the loss of a single contract but the consequences of creating and failing to meet expectations were actually much worse. The experience left the jewelry store owner convinced that radio advertising (and, likely, all other marketing mediums as well) does not work, thus poisoning the well for anyone else that might approach her for ad dollars. This result is clearly bad business.

All customers – whether they are purchasing real estate, cars or radio marketing campaigns – come away from their buying decisions carrying a set of expectations. Moreover, buyers virtually always mentally translate those expectations into at least implied promises (guarantees) from their vendors.

Salespeople must recognize that these expectations exist and use that awareness to control (shape) them early in the game. The importance of this exercise may become clearer by reviewing some of the "expectations" synonyms provided by a thesaurus which include "reliance", "presumptions", "assurance" and "trust".

At a minimum, sellers must at least meet client expectations. With that in mind, account executives will avoid the temptation to over sell, knowing their enthusiastic product description is likely to be perceived as a literal performance guarantee.

In truth, the real goal should always be to over deliver and, as a practical matter, the best way to <u>over</u> deliver is to <u>under</u> promise. Experienced sellers have learned to set the promised performance bar as low as a prospect will accept and to do so <u>before</u> closing the sale.

By allowing his client to develop the unrealistic expectation that a six-month radio advertising campaign would deliver instant results, Paul set up himself (and his radio station) to fail. And, much to his chagrin, he came off as making a lame excuse when he tried to remedy customer disappointment with an entirely reasonable explanation.

Paul was too late. But, I would argue – and I hope you'll agree – that he could have had both a nice contract and a happy client if he had just disciplined himself to assure measureable results by the end of the six-month marketing campaign.

Following The Law of Expectations is straightforward. Doing so must begin with acceptance that managing prospect expectations is critical. Then, follow some relatively simple rules.

- Recognize that customer retention will almost always depend on delivering results.
- Get the first read on prospect goals during the Client Needs Analysis with questions like: "What are your expectations from my company?" and "What would be a success?"
- With client agreement, establish realistic targets and do not accept unachievable metrics.
- Openly discuss the relationship between investment and results i.e. buying a seller's least expensive product should limit expectations.
- Only promise that which is within your control.

TWENTY

THE LAW OF RELIABILITY

Owen was the newest member of the local sales staff for a large light bulb distributor. (His employer handled everything from outdoor floodlights to the small, ornamental bulbs for decorative chandeliers.) As a rookie, Owen was expected to develop an account list from scratch and, in his case, "local" meant that he was restricted to prospecting only single-location businesses. All of the chain stores were already assigned to the company's senior sellers.

To say that Owen was "lightly" trained for his new position would be an exaggeration. His orientation began and ended with a two hour meeting with his Sales Manager during which he was given a glossy binder containing pictures and prices of all the light bulbs distributed by the company, a tool that his boss described as "self explanatory".

His supervisor devoted perhaps thirty minutes to explaining Owen's compensation plan including draw, commissions and bonus opportunities. The meeting concluded with the Sales Manager offering Owen an incredibly insightful sales training pearl of wisdom – "How much you make is directly related to how many prospects you contact each day." (If I had known it was that easy, I could have written a much shorter book.)

It was early during his second day on the job that Owen called on a small, family owned hardware business managed by Jamie, the son of the store's founder. Owen and Jamie were nearly the same age and fell into an easy conversation ranging from football to cars. Almost as an afterthought, Owen turned to the reason for his visit.

"So," he said tentatively, "Would you consider purchasing any of my company's products?"

"We can probably do some business," Jamie replied easily. He liked Owen and wanted to give the young seller a shot. "I'm running low on everyday household light bulbs. Can you help me with those?"

"Oh, that's perfect," Owen responded excitedly. He had received an e-mail from his Sales Manager just that morning *announcing a closeout special on 100-watt bulbs. "I'm going to be able to give you a discount price, too!"*

"Well then," Jamie smiled. "It looks like we have a deal."

"That's great," Owen gushed. "And you won't be sorry! I promise to stay on top of this order and give you updates on every step of the delivery process!"

"Thanks a lot," Jamie said as he shook Owen's hand. "We'll talk soon."

Owen called Jamie almost daily for the next week or so. He provided his client with updates on credit approval and contract entry. He let Jamie know when the hardware store's order reached his company's warehouse as well as when the light bulbs were packed and shipped. Finally, he reached a clerk at Jamie's business to verify that the merchandise had arrived.

Perhaps two weeks later, Owen started calling Jamie for a follow-up appointment but was unable to reach his client. After several attempts, Owen decided to visit the hardware business in person.

Jamie wasn't available at the time so Owen headed over to the store's light bulb display. He was disappointed to see that virtually all of the 100-watt bulbs he had sold were still on the shelf. Worse, he was distressed to notice a larger selection of 75-watt and 60-watt bulbs that, necessarily, had been delivered by some other vendor.

It was nearly two months after that in-store inspection that Jamie finally accepted a call from Owen. The client was cordial but declined to set another meeting with Owen, explaining that the business had decided to "go in another direction."

So, what went wrong? Most of the stories that open the chapters of this book are fairly straightforward in that, with careful review, readers can identify mistakes made by sellers. Here, finding the error is much more challenging – proof positive that The Law of Reliability is more complex than it appears on the surface.

At first blush, it would seem that Owen proved his reliability in spades. He made a promise to his client and, if anything, he over delivered on that guarantee with detailed updates on the progress of the hardware store's order. But, concluding that simply living up to a service promise satisfies the entire commitment from seller to buyer misses the mark with an interpretation of reliability that is far too narrow.

All customers depend on their sales representatives for a variety of services, both <u>express</u> and <u>implied</u>. Owen's promise to Jamie is a perfect example of the former and, for his performance, we can award Owen an "A" in the "Express" service column. And while, for lack of experience, we might be inclined to excuse Owen for not understanding the nuances of "Implied" reliability, that is small comfort to his client.

Customers will always assign professional reliability to their account executives with an expectation that such dependency is innate to the buyer-seller relationship. From the very first sales call, salespeople hold themselves out as prepared to conduct business.

With the initial handshake, sellers are essentially saying to prospects, "I am a professional. I am an expert in my field and I completely understand how my company can best serve your business. You can count on me." Whether or not that description is accurate, prospective clients implicitly trust that their sales representatives possess those qualities and enjoy the security of believing they are working with a pro.

Jamie's implied reliance on Owen was misplaced. That Jamie ended up viewing Owen as an undependable business partner is easy to understand when you consider the multiple issues which Jamie trusted Owen to understand.

- To satisfy its customers, the family owned hardware store needed to offer all standard wattages of home light bulbs, a goal not met with an order consisting of only 100-watt bulbs. For his purposes, Jamie

required a balanced distribution of 60, 75 and 100-watt bulbs, something Owen would have known had he conducted a Client Needs Analysis before closing the sale.
- Because the store was small, shelf space was at a premium. Jamie simply didn't have room to devote a large display area to only 100-watt bulbs nor would his storage closet easily accommodate the overflow. Again, this is critical information that could have been learned during a CNA.
- Like most small businesses, the hardware store's meager profits were typically used to purchase new inventory and cash was always tight. If Owen had been properly trained about his industry – knowledge for which Jamie relied on him – Owen would have been aware that 100-watt bulbs moved very, very slowly when compared to the 60 and 75-watt varieties. Instead, Jamie's limited cash flow got tied up in 100-watt inventory that would not quickly turn over.

By reading this book, existing and potential sellers have made a commitment to going beyond the training provided by their employers. I applaud that decision as proof that salespeople are not limited to only the lessons they receive from management. Sadly, Owen failed to avail himself of that opportunity and, therefore, entered the sales arena woefully unprepared to meet the implicit responsibilities attached to The Law of Reliability.

It is hardly coincidence that this chapter is placed adjacent to The Law of Expectations. While the latter represents client performance assumptions that are purposely created, the consequences (dependability, trustworthiness, security) issuing from The Law of Reliability are every bit as real. Successful salespeople must make certain they are fully prepared to accept the responsibility of being reliable business partners for their customers.

TWENTY ONE

THE LAW OF GIFTS

After six months on staff, Rick was enjoying his first sales job as an account executive for a sports apparel distributor. His company represented several major clothing brand names which were relatively easy to sell.

Rick's client list included several retail chains, most with shopping mall locations. Generally speaking, these retailers stocked at least some merchandise from every significant manufacturer including those brokered by Rick's company. Therefore, his performance was measured by the relative share of floor display space he garnered from his customers.

The buying decisions for one of Rick's larger accounts were made by the Regional Manager named Hunter. The two males bonded comfortably, a relationship based in no small part on their mutual passion for NFL football. So, when Rick's Sales Manager provided a pair of suite passes for the local pro team's first home game of the season, it was no surprise that Rick invited Hunter to be his guest.

Since his company actually owned the suite, Rick was given the same tickets for every home game, always with the proviso from his Sales Manager that the passes were "for entertaining customers". Although he certainly complied with that rule, Rick's client for each of the first four games was always Hunter. And, sure enough, Rick's contracts from Hunter's stores showed consistent growth.

That success notwithstanding, his Sales Manager sent Rick a memo after the fourth game, reminding his seller that there were other clients who deserved to be entertained. Ever the good soldier, Rick extended the suite invitation for the next game to a different customer who jumped at the opportunity.

Rick made the call to the alternate client on the Tuesday before the Sunday NFL game. That Friday, Hunter called Rick.

"Hey Partner," Hunter said collegially. "Are we doing the game together Sunday?"

"Oh wow, Hunter," Rick answered nervously, searching for the right words. "I'm afraid I made other plans this week."

"Really?" Hunter sounded genuinely surprised. "Gosh, if I had known sooner, I would have gotten tickets someplace else."

"I'm really sorry, Hunter." Rick's mind was spinning as he tried to figure out just how it was that he found himself in this position. "Please have a good weekend."

The good news is that Rick enjoyed a significant sales bump from the customer he <u>did</u> take to the game. The bad news is that the size of the orders from Hunter began to shrink. It didn't have to be that way.

It may seem trivial to devote an entire chapter to the subject of client gifts. After all, this book is supposed to be about selling – not buying – potential customers. But, that argument tends to exalt form over substance.

Let's be honest – clients love freebies! Customers with class will rarely ask for gifts, but it's the odd client who will actually turn them down. That being true, many (if not most) businesses provide their salespeople with merchandise for clients that can range from token coffee mugs with the company's logo to suite tickets to free trips.

So, with the practice of gift-giving being prevalent, it makes sense to review the considerations that can maximize the value of goodies. While doing so, I'll also raise some important warning flags.

- It's true in both personal and professional relationships – the best gifts are those that surprise the recipient, a truth that would have served our friend Rick well. By making Hunter his guest for every football game, Rick erased the "special" nature of the gift. In truth, Hunter would have had a greater appreciation for the suite opportunity if Rick had extended the invitation only a couple of times during the season. When gift-giving is smartly orchestrated, it is often the case that "less is more".

- Unless it's part of a special promotion created by the Sales Manager (and those should be rare), sellers should avoid using a gift as a "premium" only available in exchange for a client purchase. The problem with such arrangements is that they encourage customers to make a one-time buy because they want the "free" merchandise, not because they have been effectively sold on the account executive's product. This selling shortcut often makes getting renewals very challenging.
- Client gifts should not have been purchased by sellers or at least such expenditures shouldn't be obvious. (Engraved items are a good example.) Spending their own money makes account executives look somewhat desperate for business and the personal nature of such gifts is often uncomfortable for customers. In any event, this type of premium creates a precedent which cannot be sustained.
- Whenever practicable, sellers should present free customer merchandise in person. This becomes another opportunity for a non-selling ("just because") meeting which, almost certainly, will leave clients looking forward to the next visit from their account executives. At a minimum, personal delivery guarantees that gifts actually get to customers instead of getting picked off by a gate keeper.
- Finally, at the risk of stating the obvious, active accounts (those currently spending money) should get the better "stuff". In other words, sellers shouldn't waste a pair of hard-to-get concert tickets trying to get a new prospect to sign a contract.

The Law of Gifts is intended to help account executives extract strategic value from the common practice of gift-giving. But, free merchandise will never be a substitute for the exercise of strong selling fundamentals.

Discerning clients may accept goodies but they will still demand superior service. So, successful sellers will rely on good business practices and only use gifts to enhance already solid customer relationships.

TWENTY TWO

THE LAW OF MANAGERS

Dustin had served as Sales Manager for the local Midwest newspaper for nearly twenty years, a period during which he had witnessed change, change and more change. He had survived four different owners including the current, publicly traded conglomerate which also had papers in thirty other cities. And, like the entire print industry, he watched his newspaper's circulation and advertising revenue sharply decline, particularly in the last five years.

Rory was Dustin's top salesman, a status he achieved during the second of his fifteen year tenure with the paper. Many of Rory's client relationships were at least a decade old and he had managed to maintain most of his accounts as active newspaper advertisers. Rory could fairly be described as "old school", a characteristic that both helped and hurt his career.

Dustin had learned to cope with the challenges of being owned by a large national company which included having many of his superiors located back on the east coast. Most corporate communication was conducted via e-mail and his inbox stayed full of memos, the content of which ranged from new initiatives under consideration to full-on performance mandates.

For the last couple of years, Dustin was well aware that his parent company was investing a great deal of money in the development of parallel web sites for each of its owned newspapers. These internet locations were typically mirror images of their associated printed publications and, as the sites were put online, their introduction was accompanied by a corporate communiqué urging Sales Managers to monetize the new ad space.

The idea, of course, was to convince existing print clients to spend additional money for space on the newspaper's web site, a concept that many of Dustin's newer, younger sellers immediately embraced. Rory, however, wasn't buying in to the new plan.

"My customers," his protests always began, "enjoy being able to hold their print ads in their hands. You tell those corporate bean counters that the reason I always hit my budget is that I know what's best for my clients!"

Rory wasn't wrong...about his budget. He had met or exceeded his assigned quota every month for more than ten years and Dustin had been able to use that impressive performance as a defense when corporate brass noted Rory's lack of internet sales. But, times were changing.

Over recent months, the content of the company's newspaper web sites had changed dramatically. The online versions now featured articles and analysis not available in the printed papers, hundreds of additional comics and multiple slideshows of spectacular pictures.

Of more significance for Dustin and Rory, these internet improvements were coupled with a new mandate from corporate changing the structure of advertising budgets for all individual sellers. Going forward, account executives would have two monthly revenue goals, one each for the printed and online versions of their respective papers. Without exception, salespeople would be expected to achieve both budgets every month.

Dustin discussed the new revenue architecture with Rory and warned his seller of the consequences if he failed to adjust his sales strategy. Dustin's efforts, however, were met with stubborn resistance and, sure enough, Rory never came close to reaching the web site portion of his budget. In less than six months, corporate management ordered Dustin to terminate Rory's employment.

For many sellers and middle managers, these or similar circumstances would prove to be fatal to a career. But, oddly enough, this story ends at least acceptably for both of the protagonists.

Unemployed Rory was quickly hired by his market's City Business Journal and allowed to work with essentially the same client list. While his new publication also had a web site which was expected to generate independent revenue, the City Business

Journal utilized separate sales teams for print and internet sales, freeing Rory from any responsibility for the latter.

Rory's departure did cost the newspaper some print advertising dollars but the parent company was already conditioned to expect these declines so they didn't hold Dustin responsible. Meanwhile, Rory's younger replacement embraced the opportunity to sell web site ads and Dustin's superiors gave him credit for the increase in internet sales.

Yes, this chapter on The Law of Managers is last but it is certainly not least. I know what you're thinking – "Won't it be sufficient if I master the first twenty-one laws and become an excellent salesperson?" – and, philosophically, I don't disagree. But, as a practical matter, just being a good seller is often not quite enough.

The reality is that account executives must keep their bosses happy and sometimes the two parties don't have identical agendas. So, sellers must make a special effort to get tuned in to exactly what makes their superiors tick and adjust their performances accordingly. In short, salespeople must manage their managers.

"How am I doing?" The process of identifying a manager's priorities should begin with this simple question. The answer should reveal what the Sales Manager believes are a seller's weaknesses and provides a clear path for the salesperson to address the negative perception.

Use sales meetings to help identify a manager's hot buttons. If the boss returns to the same or similar topic repeatedly, a salesperson must be willing to take the hint.

Match passion with passion. Which ideas get the Sales Manager excited? If the superior is passionate about a particular selling process, the seller should make the effort to mirror that enthusiasm.

Be creative in communication with the boss because Sales Managers rarely appreciate salespeople who are defensive or argumentative. Recognize that "Do you think we should consider offering a discount to encourage this prospect to buy?" is much more likely to elicit a constructive response than just telling the manager that "Our prices are too high so this prospect won't buy."

The challenge presented by The Law of Managers is to eliminate the apparent conflict between the following two statements. First, because Sales Managers have ultimate authority, sellers must acknowledge priorities established by their leaders. Second, talented salespeople should never let their performance be crippled by the demands of management. While both statements are true, marrying their divergent implications requires special effort.

The solution to this problem is found in that old adage – "Perception is reality." While Sales Managers deserve more respect than to have their ideas addressed by only smoke and mirrors, sellers can nevertheless usually keep their superiors happy by offering equal measures of attention and effort.

It's easy enough for account executives to demonstrate that they are listening to the boss. Parroting back what they have heard or asking for clarification are both good examples. When Sales Managers are satisfied that their sellers are paying attention, they are more likely to perceive that their employees are following through with activity.

I must hasten to point out that nothing in this chapter should be interpreted to undermine the legitimacy of management. Sales Managers DO have many good ideas and they DO provide salespeople with important direction. All sellers require solid leadership in order to grow their skills.

Rather, the focus here is on the relationship between employers and employees as perceived by the former. Good salespeople – even those who achieve their budgets every month – can jeopardize their careers by failing to accommodate the priorities of their managers. It goes with the territory – accomplished sellers will maximize their professional longevity only by learning to manage their managers!

www.ingramcontent.com/pod-product-compliance
Lightning Source LLC
Chambersburg PA
CBHW072017200526
45171CB00013B/132